Charles Duke Yonge

The Accidence

First Rudiments of the Latin Tongue

Charles Duke Yonge

The Accidence
First Rudiments of the Latin Tongue

ISBN/EAN: 9783743393707

Manufactured in Europe, USA, Canada, Australia, Japa

Cover: Foto ©Paul-Georg Meister /pixelio.de

Manufactured and distributed by brebook publishing software (www.brebook.com)

Charles Duke Yonge

The Accidence

THE ACCIDENCE,

OR

FIRST RUDIMENTS

OF THE

LATIN TONGUE,

BEING THE FIRST PART OF THE NEW ETON LATIN GRAMMAR

(TO THE END OF THREE CONCORDS,)

BY C. D. YONGE, B.A.

AUTHOR OF
"AN ENGLISH-GREEK LEXICON," "YONGE'S GRADUS AD PARNASSUM,"
ETC. ETC.

ETON: WILLIAMS & SON;
LONDON: SIMPKIN, MARSHALL, AND Co.

MDCCCLXXIII.

INDEX.

	Pag.
Alphabet	5
Parts of Speech	6
NOUNS—	
Numbers, Cases, &c.	ib.
Declension of Substantives	8
,, Adjectives	15
Comparison of Adjectives	19
Pronouns	21
Declension of	22
VERBS—	
Voices	24
Moods	25
Tenses	26
Gerunds and Supines	27
Participles	ib.
Numbers and Persons	28
The Verb *Esse*	ib.
Declension of Verbs *Regular*	31
Conjugation of ditto—Active	32
,, ,, Passive	45
Declension of *Irregular* Verbs	58
Conjugation of ditto	ib.
Defective Verbs	63
Adverbs	65
Conjunctions	ib.
Prepositions	66
Interjections	68
The Three Concords	ib.
PROPRIA QUÆ MARIBUS; or, the Genders of Nouns	73

	Pag.
QUÆ GENUS; or, Nouns Heteroclite	77
AS IN PRÆSENTI; or, the Perfect and Supines of Verbs	80
SYNTAXIS—	
Concordantiæ Tres	88
Nominum Constructio—	
Substantiva	92
Adjectiva	93
Pronominum Constructio	98
Verborum Constructio	99
Verba Infinita	107
Gerundia	109
Supina	110
Verba Impersonalia	ib.
De Tempore	111
Spatium Loci	112
Nomina Locorum	ib.
Adverbiorum Constructio	113
Conjunctionum Constructio	114
De Relativo	118
Præpositionum Constructio	119
Interjectionum Constructio	121
PROSODIA	122
Propria quæ Maribus construed	132
Nouns Heteroclite construed	140
As in Præsenti construed	144
Syntaxis construed	157
Prosodia construed	206

AN INTRODUCTION
TO THE
LATIN TONGUE.

The Latin Letters are thus written:
Capitals.
A B C D E F G H I J K L M N O P Q R S T U V X Y Z.
Small, or common.
a b c d e f g h i j k l m n o p q r s t u v x y z.

Of these Letters, six are named *Vowels; a, e, i, o, u, y.*
The rest are called *consonants.*

A *vowel* makes a full and perfect sound of itself, as *e.*

A *consonant* cannot be sounded without a vowel, as *be.*

Consonants are divided into liquids, double letters, and mutes.

The *liquids* are *l, m, n, r :* The *double letters* are *j, x, z :* The remaining letters are called *mutes.*

A *syllable* is a distinct sound of one, or more letters, pronounced in a breath.

A *diphthong* is the sound of two vowels in one syllable. There are six diphthongs, *ae, ai, au, ei, eu, oe.**

---

* Besides these six we meet with *ua, ue, ui, uo,* sounded in one syllable, occurring only after the consonants, *g, q,* or *s;* but they want one distinguishing property of diphthongs, for diphthongs are naturally *long* in quantity, while these are sometimes long and sometimes short. And some consider that in these combinations *u* should be considered a consonant, and written *v.*

PARTS OF SPEECH.

The Parts of Speech are Seven:
Noun, Pronoun, Verb, declined;
Adverb, Conjunction, Preposition, Interjection, undeclined.

OF A NOUN.

NOUNS are of two kinds, *Substantives* and *Adjectives*.

A *substantive* expresses by itself alone the object of which we are speaking; as, *hŏmo*,* a man; *ōrātor*, an orator; *līber*, the book.

An *adjective* always requires to be joined to a substantive, of which it shows the nature or quality; and is either a common adjective; as, *bŏnus puer*, a good boy; or a *participle* (formed from, and being part of a verb); as, *fŭrens fœmĭna*, a woman raging.

NUMBERS OF NOUNS.

NOUNS have two numbers; the singular, and the plural.

The singular speaketh but of one; as *pătĕr*, a father

The plural speaketh of more than one; as, *patres*, fathers.

CASES OF NOUNS.

NOUNS have six cases in each number:

The nominative, the genitive, the dative, the accusative, the vocative, and the ablative.

The *nominative* case names the subject of a sentence, and marks the quarter from which an action proceeds; as, *magister docet*, the master teaches.

The *genitive* case denotes connection between two objects, and in English is commonly translated by *"of,"* or by *'s*; as, *doctrina magistri*, the learning of the master, or the master's learning.

The *dative* case denotes that with reference to which the subject (named by the nominative case) acts; or in

---

* A crescent (˘) placed over a vowel denotes that the syllable is *short*; a straight line (¯) denotes that it is *long*.

reference to which it possesses this or that quality: and in English it is commonly expressed by the sign "*to*" or "*for*," pointing out the person to whose advantage or disadvantage the thing spoken of tends; as, *do librum magistro,* I give the book to the master; *patriæ suæ idoneus,* useful to his country.

The *accusative* case expresses the object, whether person or thing, affected by the action spoken of; as, *amo magistrum,* I love the master; *condo domum,* I build a house.

The *vocative* case is used in addressing people or things; as, *O magister,* O master.

The *ablative* case serves to denote the person or thing from whom or from which anything is taken; and also many other relations of substantives, which are expressed in most other languages by prepositions, such as, "*in,*" "*with,*" "*from,*" or "*by.*" Also, the word "*than*" after an adjective of the comparative degree is often a sign of the ablative case; as, *cum magistro,* with the master; *in Italiâ,* in Italy; *vir fortior Cæsare,* a man braver than Cæsar.

GENDERS AND ARTICLES.

The GENDERS of nouns are three; the masculine, the feminine, and the neuter.

Some substantives are called *common*, being such as denote an occupation or quality common to both males and females, and admitting adjectives of either the masculine or feminine gender to be joined with them, according as the subject is male or female; as, *meus parens,* or *mea parens,* "my parent," according as the father or mother is spoken of.

Some are called *epicene*, being such as have only one grammatical gender, which comprehends both sexes; as, *hic passer,* this sparrow; *hæc aquila,* this eagle; without regard to the difference of sex.

Some are called *doubtful,* being such as are sometimes masculine and sometimes feminine, without regard to the actual sex of the animal spoken of; as, *hic anguis* or *hæc anguis,* this snake.

DECLENSION OF NOUNS SUBSTANTIVE.

There are FIVE declensions of substantives, distinguished by the ending of the genitive case.

THE FIRST DECLENSION.

The First declension makes the genitive case singular to end in *æ*, and has the nominative case ending in *ă*, of either the masculine or feminine gender; as, *scrība*, a scribe; *via*, a way; or, (in the case of words derived from Greek, being mostly proper names) in *as* or *es* of the masculine, and in *ē* of the feminine gender. These last make the genitive singular to end in *ēs*.

Singular.	Plural.
N. Mūs-a, *a song*,	N. Mūs-æ, *songs*,
G. Mūs-æ, *of a song*,*	G. Mūs-ārum, *of songs*,
D. Mūs-æ, *to a song*,	D. Mūs-is, *to songs*,
Acc. Mūs-am, *a song*,	A. Mūs-as, *songs*,
V. Mūs-a, *o song*,	V. Mūs-æ, *o songs*,
Abl. Mūs-â, *from a song*.	A. Mūs-is, *from songs*.

N. Ænēas,	Anchīses,	Pēnĕlŏpē,
G. Ænēæ,	Anchīsæ,	Pēnĕlŏpēs,
D. Ænēæ,	Anchīsæ,	Pēnĕlŏpæ,
Acc. Ænēān,	Anchīsēn,	Pēnĕlŏpēn,
V. Ænēā,	Anchīsā,†	Pēnĕlŏpē,
Abl. Ænēâ.	Anchīsâ.	Pēnĕlŏpē.

One or two feminine substantives in *ă*, derived from masculines in *us*, make the dat. and abl. plural in *ābus* as well as in *is*; as, *filia*, a daughter, *filiabus* or *filiis*.

Also feminine proper names ending in *ă*, derived from the Greek, are used in Latin (especially by the poets) with either accusative *an* or *am*; and *an*, when used, follows the quantity of the Greek accusative, so that we find *Maiăn, Electrān*.

---

* The Epic Poets occasionally retain the older form, which used to end in *aï*; as, *Aulaï* in medio, for *Aulæ*. Virg.

† Horace in his Satires uses this vocative case with *ă*.

THE SECOND DECLENSION.

The second declension makes the genitive case singular to end in *i*, and the nominative to end in *ĕr* and *ĭr* of the masculine gender only; as, *puer*, a boy; *măgister*, a teacher; *vir*, a man: in *us*, usually of the masculine gender; as, *dŏmĭnus*, a master; but sometimes of the feminine; as, *hŭmus*, the ground; or of the neuter, as, *vīrus*,* poison: in *um* of the neuter gender only; as, *regnum*, a kingdom: and (in the case of a few proper names derived from the Greek) in *ŏs* of the masculine or feminine gender, as, *Dēlŏs*; and in *ŏn* of the neuter, as, *Iliŏn*.

Singular.
N. Puer, *a boy*,
G. Puĕri, *of a boy*,
D. Puĕro, *to a boy*,
A. Puĕrum, *a boy*,
V. Puer, *o boy*,
A. Puĕro, *by a boy*.

Plural.
N. Puĕri, *boys*,
G. Puĕrōrum, *of boys*,
D. Puĕris, *to boys*,
A. Puĕros, *boys*,
V. Puĕri, *o boys*,
A. Puĕris, *by boys*.

Singular.
N. Dŏmĭnus, *a master*,
G. Dŏmĭni, *of a master*,
D. Dŏmĭno, *to a master*,
A. Dŏmĭnum, *a master*,
V. Dŏmĭne, *o master*,
A. Dŏmĭno, *by a master*.

Plural.
N. Dŏmĭni, *masters*,
G. Dŏmĭnōrum, *of masters*,
D. Dŏmĭnis, *to masters*,
A. Dŏmĭnos, *masters*,
V. Dŏmĭni, *o masters*,
A. Dŏmĭnis, *by masters*.

Singular.
N. Măgister, *a teacher*,
G. Măgistri, *of a teacher*,
D. Măgistro, *to a teacher*,
A. Măgistrum, *a teacher*,
V. Măgister, *o teacher*,
A. Măgistro, *by a teacher*.

Plural.
N. Măgistri, *teachers*,
G. Măgistrōrum, *of teachers*,
D. Măgistris, *to teachers*,
A. Măgistros, *teachers*,
V. Măgistri, *o teachers*,
A. Măgistris, *by teachers*.

---

* Nouns of the neuter gender of this declension ending in *us* make the accusative and vocative singular to end in *us*, and have no plural; except that Lucretius has *Pĕlăgē* as the accusative plural of *Pĕlăgus*.

Singular.	Plural.
N. Regn-um, *a kingdom,*	N. Regn-a, *kingdoms,*
G. Regn-i, *of a kingdom,*	G. Regn-ōrum, *of kingdoms*
D. Regn-o, *to a kingdom,*	D. Regn-is, *to kingdoms,*
A. Regn-um, *a kingdom,*	A. Regn-a, *kingdoms,*
V. Regn-um, *o kingdom,*	V. Regn-a, *o kingdoms,*
A. Regn-o, *from a kingdom.*	A. Regn-is, *from kingdoms.*
N. Dēlŏs,	Iliŏn,
G. Dēli,	Ilii,
D. Dēlo,	Ilio,
A. Dēlŏn,	Iliŏn,
V. Dēlĕ,	Iliŏn,
A. Dēlo.	Ilio.

The genitive case of words ending in *ius* or *ium* was originally *î*, not *ii*, and *ii* is never used by Virgil or Horace (except in the case of the adjective *ēgrĕgii,)* though it occurs occasionally in Ovid.

The vocative of words ending in *us* terminates in *e*, except *Deus*, God, which makes *Deus* in the vocative; and words in *ius*, which make the vocative in *i;* as, *filius*, a son, *filî*. But proper names derived from the Greek ending in *ius* make the vocative in *e;* as, *Cynthius*, *Cynthie*.

All nouns of the neuter gender have the nominative, accusative, and vocative cases alike in both numbers. And all nouns whatever, except those of the first declension ending in *as* or *es*, and those of the second ending in *us* or *ŏs*, make the nominative and vocative alike in both numbers.

THE THIRD DECLENSION.

The third declension makes the genitive case singular to end in *is*, and in the nominative it ends in *e, o* (and in words derived from the Greek in *a, i,* and *y,*) *c, l, n, r, s, t,* and *x*, of which those ending in *a, e, i, y, c, t,* are of the neuter gender only (except *Præneste*, which, as the name of a town, is used also in the feminine.) Those with the other terminations are of various genders, except that those ending in *o, ns,* and *x*, are never neuter.

Of nouns of this declension some are *parisyllabic*
(that is, they do not increase in the genitive case,) as,
nūbes, nūbis; some are *imparisyllabic* (that is, they do
increase in the genitive case,) as, *lapis, lapĭdis.** Some

---

* In the case of imparisyllabic words, there is a great variety in the manner in which the increase in the genitive case is formed: the following are some of the principal varieties. Words ending in—

a	make the gen. in ătis, *as* poēma, poemătis.
o		ĭnis, *as* virgo, virgĭnis.
		ōnis, *as* leo, leōnis.
		ŏnis, *as* Măcĕdo, Măcĕdŏnis.
y		yŏs, *as* Tīphys, Tīphyŏs.
c		ctis, *as* lac, lactis.
l		lis, *as* ănĭmal, ănĭmālis; sal, sălis; mel, mellis.
	an	ānis, *as* Tītān, Tītānis.
	ēn	ēnis, *as* Sīrēn, Sīrēnis.
n	in	īnis, *as* Delphīn, Delphīnis.
	ĕn	ĭnis, *as* carmĕn, carmĭnis.
	ōn	ōnis, *as* Mărăthon, Mărăthōnis.
		ŏnis, *as* cănōn, cănŏnis.
		ontis, *as* Xenophon, Xenophontis.
r	by adding is, *as* calcar, calcāris.
		jŭbar, jubăris.
		carcer, carcĕris.
		ver, vēris.
		hŏnor, hŏnōris.
		æquor, æquŏris.
		fur, fūris.
		murmur, murmŭris; but far makes farris; ĭter, ĭtĭnĕris; Jūpĭter, Jŏvis; cor, cordis; rōbur, rōbŏris.
as	in ātis, *as* pietās, pietātis:

but in words derived from the Greek—
in ădis, *as* lampăs, lampădis.
antis, *as* gīgas, gigantis.
We find also mas, măris; vas, vāsis; vas, vădis; as, assis.
ĕs in ītis, *as* mīlĕs, mīlĭtis.
ĕs in ĕtis, *as* sĕgĕs, sĕgĕtis.
· We find also quies, quiētis; pes, pĕdis; hæres, hærēdis; Cĕrĕs, Cĕrēris.
is in ĕris, *as* cĭnis, cĭnĕris.
ĭdis, *as* lapis, lăpĭdis.
We find also līs, lītis; sanguis, sanguĭnis; glīs, glīris.

ns } by changing *s* into *tis*, { *as* părens, părentis.
rs }   ars, artis.

So also we find trabs, trăbis; urbs, urbis; hyems, hyĕmis; cœlebs, cœlĭbis; princeps, princĭpis; but frons (a leaf,) frondis; glans, glandis.

parisyllabic nouns ending in *is* make the accusative case singular to end in *im*,* as, *turris, turrim*; and these and some others make the ablative to end both in *i* and *e*, as, *puppis*, abl. *puppi* and *puppe* (one, *vis*, makes only *vi*.) All nouns of the neuter gender form their nominative, accusative, and vocative plural in *a;* those which end in *al, ar* (except *far*,) and *e*, make them in *ia*. And such words, and most parisyllabic substantives of this declension, form their genitive case plural in *ium*.†

Words ending in
ŭs make the gen. in ōris, *as* flōs, flōris.
    ōtis, *as* dos, dōtis.
      also os (a bone,) ossis.
    oïs, *as* heros (borrowed from the Greek,) herois.
us, when neut. in ĕris, *as* ŏpus, ŏpĕris.
    ŏris, *as* pĕcus, pĕcŏris.
 when fem. in ūtis, *as* virtūs, virtūtis.
    ŭdis, *as* pĕcus, pĕcŭdis.
We find also Vĕnus, Vĕnĕris; grus, gruis : and the masculine mus, mūris.
x   in cis, *as* pax, pācis.
    fax, făcis.
    vervex, vervĕcis,
    nex, nĕcis.
    cornix, cornīcis.
    călix, călĭcis.
    vox, vōcis.
    Cappădox, Cappădŏcis.
    lux, lūcis.
    nux, nŭcis.
    lynx, lyncis.

But *ex* makes also ĭcis, *as* lătex, lătĭcis; we find also rex, rĕgis; grex, grĕgis; rēmex, rēmĭgis; nix, nĭvis; nox, noctis; Phryx, Phrўgis.

* Some, being chiefly Greek proper names, make the accusative singular in *ĭn*, as *Păris, Părĭn*, and these make the vocative in *ĭ*, as *Părĭ*. Some imparisyllabic words also, derived from the Greek, being chiefly proper names, make the accusative singular to end in *ă;* and if they have a plural number, the plural nominative ends in *ĕs*, and the accusative in *ăs*, as *Pallăs*, the goddess, *Pallădă; Pallăs*, the man, *Pallanta; lampăs*, acc. sing. *lampăda*, nom. and voc. pl. *lampădĕs*, acc. *lampădăs*. These words also sometimes are used by the poets with the dative case plural in *ăsĭn*, as *Trŏăs*, a Trojan woman, *Trŏădă. Trŏădĕs, Trŏăsĭn, Trŏădăs.*

† *Vātes, sĕnex, jŭvĕnis, ăpis, cănis, vŏlŭcris*, are exceptions to this rule, and form their genitive plural in *ium*, not in *ium*. Most nouns of one syllable make the genitive plural in *um;* those of two or more syllables ending in *ns* or *rs*, make it both in *ium* and *um*. the former being the most common form in prose.

Proper names ending in *as, antis,* make the vocative case singular to end in *ā,* as *Calchas, Calchantis,* voc. *Calchā ;* and those in *es, is,* make it *ēs* and in *ē,* and make the accusative in *em* or in *ēn;* as, *Sophocles, Sophoclis,* accus. *Sophoclem* or *Sophoclen,* voc. *Sophocles* or *Sophoclē.*

Singular.
N. Nŭbes, *a cloud,*
G. Nŭbis, *of a cloud,*
D. Nŭbi, *to a cloud,*
A. Nŭbem, *a cloud,*
V. Nŭbes, *o cloud,*
A. Nŭbe, *by a cloud.*

Plural.
N. Nŭbes, *clouds,*
G. Nŭbium, *of clouds,*
D. Nŭbĭbus, *to clouds,*
A. Nŭbes, *clouds,*
V. Nŭbes, *o clouds,*
A. Nŭbĭbus, *by clouds.*

Singular.
N. Lăpis, *a stone,*
G. Lăpĭdis, *of a stone,*
D. Lăpĭdi, *to a stone,*
A. Lăpĭdem, *a stone,*
V. Lăpis, *o stone,*
A. Lăpĭde, *by a stone.*

Plural.
N. Lăpĭdes, *stones,*
G. Lăpĭdum, *of stones,*
D. Lăpĭdĭbus, *to stones,*
A. Lăpĭdes, *stones,*
V. Lăpĭdes, *o stones,*
A. Lăpĭdĭbus, *by stones.*

Singular.
N. ŏpus, *a work,*
G. ŏpĕris, *of a work,*
D. ŏpĕri, *to a work,*
A. ŏpus, *a work,*
V. ŏpus, *o work,*
A. ŏpĕre, *by a work.*

Plural.
N. ŏpĕra, *works,*
G. ŏpĕrum, *of works,*
D. ŏpĕrĭbus, *to works,*
A. ŏpĕra, *works,*
V. ŏpĕra, *o works,*
A. ŏpĕrĭbus, *by works.*

Singular.
N. Măre, *a sea,*
G. Măris, *of a sea,*
D. Mări, *to a sea,*
A. Măre, *a sea,*
V. Măre, *o sea,*
A. Mări, or Măre, *by the sea.*

Plural.
N. Măria, *seas,*
G. Mărium, *of seas,*
D. Mărĭbus, *to seas,*
A. Măria, *seas,*
V. Măria, *o seas,*
A. Mărĭbus, *by seas.*

Besides these words, there are some proper names derived from the Greek, which belong mainly to the second declension, but have some cases (especially in poetry) which belong to the third:

B

N. Orpheus,
G. Orphei, or Orpheŏs,
D. Orpheo, or Orphĕī, contr. Orphē,
A. Orpheum, or Orphĕă, contr. Orphae,
V. Orpheu,
A. Orpheo.

Sappho is thus declined:

N. Sappho,
G. Sapphûs,
D. Sappho,
A. Sappho,
V. Sappho,
A. Sappho.

THE FOURTH DECLENSION.

The fourth declension makes the genitive case singular to end in *ûs*, and in the nominative ends in *us*, being of either the masculine or feminine gender; or in *u*, of the neuter gender.

Singular.	Plural.
N. Grăd-us, *a step*,	N. Grăd-us, *steps*,
G. Grăd-ûs, *of a step*,	G. Grăd-uum, *of steps*,
D. Grăd-ui, *to a step*,	D. Grăd-ĭbus, *to steps*,
A. Grăd-um, *a step*,	A. Grăd-us, *steps*,
V. Grăd-us, *o step*,	V. Grăd-us, *o steps*,
A. Grăd-u, *with a step*.	A. Grăd-ĭbus, *with steps*.

The dative in *ui* is sometimes contracted into *ú*, both in poetry and prose, as, *Parce metú.*—Virg.

Singular.	Plural.
N. Cornu, *a horn*,	N. Cornua, *horns*,
G. Cornûs, *of a horn*,*	G. Cornuum, *of horns*,
D. Cornui, *to a horn*,*	D. Cornĭbus, *to horns*,
A. Cornu, *a horn*,	A. Cornua, *horns*,
V. Cornu, *o horn*,	V. Cornua, *o horns*,
A. Cornu, *with a horn*.	A. Cornĭbus, *with horns*.

Dŏmus, a house, belongs partly to the fourth declension and partly to the second.

---

* But the genitive and dative cases singular of words in *u* are scarcely ever found.

Singular.	Plural.
N. Dŏmus, *a house,*	N. Dŏmus, *houses,*
G. Dŏmûs, *of a house,*	G. Dŏmuum *and* dŏmorum, *of houses,*
D. Dŏmui & dŏmo, *to a house,*	D. Dŏmĭbus, *to houses,*
A. Dŏmum, *a house,*	A. Dŏmos, *houses,*
V. Dŏmus, *o house,*	V. Dŏmųs, *o houses,*
A. Dŏmo, *by a house.*	A. Dŏmĭbus, *by houses.*

THE FIFTH DECLENSION.

The fifth declension makes the genitive and dative cases singular to end in *ei,* and in the nominative ends in *es,* being always of the feminine gender, with the exception of *dies,* a day, which is masculine and feminine in the singular, and only masculine in the plural; as,

Singular.	Plural.
N. Făci-es, *a face,*	N. Făci-es, *faces,*
G. Făci-ēi, *of a face,*	G. Făci-ērum, *of faces,*
D. Făci-ēi, *to a face,*	D. Făci-ēbus, *to faces,*
A. Făci-em, *a face,*	A. Făci-es, *faces,*
V. Făci-es, *o face,*	V. Făci-es, *o faces,*
A. Făci-ē, *from a face.*	A. Făci-ēbus, *from faces.*

The termination of the genitive singular in *ei* is sometimes contracted in poetry into *é;* as, " Libra *dié* somnique pares ubi fecerit horas."—Virg.

DECLENSION OF NOUNS ADJECTIVE.

Adjectives are declined like substantives, and have either three terminations, masculine, feminine, and neuter; or two, the one masculine and feminine, and the other neuter; or one termination only, serving for the three genders. Most adjectives of three terminations are declined in the masculine and neuter genders, like substantives of the second declension, and in the feminine like substantives of the first declension; as, *bŏnus,* good; *tĕner,* tender; *āter,* black.

B 2

	Singular.			Plural.		
	M.	F.	N.	M.	F.	N.
N.	Bŏn-us,	bon-a,	bon-um,	Bŏn-i,	bon-æ,	bon-a,
G.	Bon-i,	bon-æ,	bon-i,	Bon-órum,	bon-árum,	bon-
D.	Bon-o,	bon-æ,	bon-o,	Bon-is,		[órum,
A.	Bon-um,	bon-am,	bon-um,	Bon-os,	bon-as,	bon-a,
V.	Bon-e,	bon-a,	bon-um,	Bon-i,	bon-æ,	bon-a,
A.	Bon-o,	bon-â,	bon-o.	Bon-is.		

Meus, mine, makes in the vocative case sing. mas. *meus*, and *mî*,* not *mee*.

	Singular.			Plural.		
	M.	F.	N.	M.	F.	N.
N.	Tĕn-er,	tenĕ-ra,	tenĕ-rum,	Tene-ri,	tene-ræ,	tene-ra,
G.	Tene-ri,	tene-ræ,	tene-ri,	Tene-rórum,	tene-rárum,	
D.	Tene-ro,	tene-ræ,	tene-ro,	Tene-ris,		[tene-rórum,
A.	Tene-rum,	-ram,	-rum,	Tene-ros,	tene-ras,	tene-ra,
V.	Ten-er,	tene-ra,	tene-rum,	Tene-ri,	tene-ræ,	tene-ra,
A.	Tene-ro,	tene-râ,	tene-ro.	Tene-ris.		

	Singular.			Plural.		
	M.	F.	N.	M.	F.	N.
N.	Āter,	atra,	atrum,	Atri,	atræ,	atra,
G.	Atri,	atræ,	atri,	Atrorum,	atrarum,	atrorum,
D.	Atro,	atræ,	atro,	Atris,		
A.	Atrum,	atram,	atrum,	Atros,	atras,	atra,
V.	Ater,	atra,	atrum,	Atri,	atræ,	atra,
A.	Atro,	atrâ,	atro.	Atris.		

Some adjectives in *er*, however, are declined in all the three genders like substantives of the third declension; as, *ācer*, active.

	Singular.			Plural.		
	M.	F.	N.	M.	F.	N.
N.	Ăcer,	acris,	acre,	Acres,	acres,	acria,
G.	Acris,			Acrium,		
D.	Acri,			Acrĭbus,		
A.	Acrem,	acrem,	acre,	Acres,	acres,	acria,
V.	Acer,	acris,	acre,	Acres,	acres,	acria,
A.	Acri.			Acrĭbus.		

* *Mî* in the inferior Authors is occasionally used for the vocative of any gender of either number.

Unus one, *solus* alone, *totus* the whole, *ullus* any, *nullus* none, *alter** the other, *uter* whether of the two, make the genitive case singular in *ius*, and the dative in *i*; as,†

Singular.

	M.	F.	N.
N.	Ūn-us,	un-a,	un-um,
G.	Un-īus,		
D.	Un-ī,		
A.	Un-um,	un-am,	un-um,
V.	Un-e,	un-a,	un-um,
A.	Un-o,	un-â,	un-o.

Plural.

	M.	F.	N.
N.	Un-i,	un-æ,	un-a,
G.	Un-órum,	-árum,	órum,
D.	Un-is,		
A.	Un-os,	un-as,	un-a,
V.	Un-i,	un-æ,	un-a,
A.	Un-is.		

Note. *Unus* has no plural number, unless it be joined to a noun that has not the singular number; as, *unæ literæ*, a letter; *una mœnia*, a wall.

Adjectives of two terminations are declined like substantives of the third declension; as, *tristis* sad, *melior* better.

Singular.

	M.F.	N.
N.	Trist-is,	trist-e,
G.	Trist-is,	
D.	Trist-i,	
A.	Trist-em,	trist-e,
V.	Trist-is,	trist-e,
A.	Trist-i, *very rarely* tristē.‡	

Plural.

	M.F.	N.
N.	Trist-es,	trist-ia,
G.	Trist-ium,	
D.	Trist-ïbus,	
A.	Trist-es,	trist-ia,
V.	Trist-es,	trist-ia,
A.	Trist-ïbus.	

---

* *Alteræ* is also used as the dat. sing. fem. of *alter*, by Corn. Nepos.

† So also words compounded of *uter*, as *neuter*, neither; *uterque*, each, fem. *utraque*, neut. *utrumque*. *Alius*, another, also makes *ălīus* in the genitive case, *alīī* dat.; it also makes *ăliud*, nom. and acc. sing. neut.

‡ There are in poetry a few instances of adjectives in *is* making the ablative in *e*, but they are very rare; and in adjectives of one termination, the ablative usually ends in *i*, except in words ending in *x*, increasing short, or in *ens* or *ans*, whose ablative most commonly ends in *e*, though *i* also is found, and except *pauper, senex, juvenis*, and *princeps*, and adjectives ending in *ĕs*, as *sŭperstĕs*, which make the ablative in *e* only.

B 3

Singular.	Plural.
M.F. N.	M.F. N.
N. Mĕli-or, mĕli-us,	N. Mĕli-ōres, meli-ōra,
G. Mĕli-ōris,	G. Mĕli-ōrum,
D. Mĕli-ōri,	D. Mĕli-ōrĭbus,
A. Mĕli-ōrem, mĕli-us,	A. Mĕli-ōres, mĕli-ōra,
V. Mĕli-or, mĕli-us,	V. Mĕli-ōres, mĕli-ōra,
A. Mĕli-ōre, *or* mĕli-ōri.	A. Mĕli-ōrĭbus.

Adjectives of one termination, which however two in acc. sing. and in nom. acc. and voc. p. also declined like substantives of the third declensi *felix* happy, *ingens* vast.—And some have no n gender at all, except in particular cases, of whicl most common are the dat. and abl. sing. and have : any distinctive neuter termination; as, *memor* mii *sŭperstĕs* surviving.

Singular.	Plural.
M.F. N.	M.F. N.
N. Fēl-ix,	N. Fēlī-ces, fēlī-cia,
G. Fēlī-cis,	G. Fēlī-cium,
D. Fēlī-ci,	D. Fēlī-cĭbus,
A. Fēlī-cem, fēl-ix,	A. Fēlī-ces, fēlī-cia,
V. Fēl-ix,	V. Fēlī-ces, fēlī-cia,
A. Fēlī-ci, *or* feli-ce.	A. Fēlī-cĭbus.

Singular.	Plural.
M.F. N.	M.F. N.
N. Ingens,	N. Ingentes, ingentia,
G. Ingentis,	G. Ingentium,
D. Ingenti,	D. Ingentĭbus,
A. Ingentem, ingens,	A. Ingentes, ingentia,
V. Ingens,	V. Ingentes, ingentia,
A. Ingenti, *or* ingente.	A. Ingentĭbus.

Singular.	Plural.
N. Mĕmor,	N. Mĕmōres,
G. Memŏris,	G. Mĕmŏrum,
D. Mĕmŏri,	D. Mĕmŏrĭbus,
A. Mĕmŏrem,	A. Mĕmōres,
V. Mĕmor,	V. Mĕmōres,
A. Mĕmŏre, *or* mĕmŏri.	A. Mĕmŏribus.

Ambo both, and *duo* two, are nouns adjective, and are thus declined, in the plural number only:

N. Amb-o,	amb-æ,	amb-o,	*both.*
G. Amb-ōrum,	amb-ārum,	amb-ōrum,	*of both.*
D. Amb-ōbus,	amb-ābus,	amb-ōbus,	*to both.*
A. Amb-os,	amb-as,	amb-o,	*both.*
V. Amb-o,	amb-æ,	amb-o,	*both.*
A. Amb-ōbus,	amb-ābus,	amb-ōbus,	*with both.*

COMPARISON OF ADJECTIVES.

Adjectives have three degrees of signification, or comparison; the positive, the comparative, and the superlative:

I. The positive denotes the quality of a thing absolutely; as, *doctus* learned, *brĕvis* short.

II. The comparative increases, or lessens the quality; as, *doctior* more learned, *brĕvior* shorter, or more short:
And it is formed of the first case of the positive that endeth in *i*, by adding thereto *or* in the masculine and feminine genders, and *us* in the neuter; as, of
Doctus, gen. *docti*, is formed *doctior*, more learned: of
Brĕvis, dat. *brĕvi*, is formed *brĕvior*, shorter.

III. The superlative increases, or diminishes the signification, or comparison, to the greatest degree; as, *doctissimus* most learned, or very learned; *brevissimus* shortest, most short, or very short:
And it is formed also of the first case of the positive that endeth in *i*, by adding thereto *ssĭmus*; as, of
Gen. *docti*, is formed *doctissĭmus*, most learned.
Dat. *brĕvi*, is formed *brĕvissĭmus*, shortest.

Note. Many Adjectives vary from these general rules, and form their comparisons irregularly; as,

Bŏnus,	good;	*mĕlior,*	better;	*optĭmus,*	best.
Mălus,	bad;	*pējor,*	worse;	*pessĭmus,*	worst.
Magnus,	great;	*mājor,*	greater;	*maxĭmus,*	greatest.
Parvus,	little;	*mĭnor,*	less;	*mĭnĭmus,*	least.
Multus,	much;	*plus,*	more;	*plūrĭmus,*	most.

Nĕquam, wicked; *nēquior*, more wicked; *nēquissĭmus*, most wicked.
Dīves, rich; *dīvĭtior*, or *dītior*, more rich; *dīvĭtissĭmus*, or *dītissĭmus*, most rich.
Extĕrus, outward; *extĕrior*, more outward; *extrēmus*, and *extĭmus*, uttermost, or most outward.
Infĕrus, low; *infĕrior*, lower, or more low; *infĭmus*, and *ĭmus*, lowest, or most low.
Sŭpĕrus, high; *sŭpĕrior*, higher, or more high; *suprēmus*, or *summus*, highest, or most high.
Postĕrus, subsequent; *postĕrior*, later; *postrēmus*, last.
Dexter, on the right hand; *dextĕrior*, *dextĭmus*, both in nearly the same sense as the positive.
Jŭvĕnis, young; *jūnior*, younger, or more young.
Sĕnex, old; *sĕnior*, older, or more old.

Adjectives in -*dĭcus*, -*fĭcus*, -*vŏlus*, derived from the verbs *dico, facio, volo*, form their comparisons in -*entior* and -*entissimus*, as if from the present participle of these verbs; as,

Maledicus, inclined to speak ill, *maledicentior*, *maledicentissimus*.
Beneficus, inclined to do good, *beneficentior*, *beneficentissimus*.
Benevolus, wishing well, *benevolentior*, *benevolentissimus*.

Some adjectives in the comparative and superlative degrees are formed from prepositions; as, from

Intra, within; *intĕrior*, inner; *intĭmus*, inmost.
Ultra, beyond; *ultĕrior*, further; *ultĭmus*, furthest, last.
Citra, on this side; *citĕrior*, nearer; *citĭmus*, nearest.
Prope, near; *prŏpior*, nearer; *proxĭmus*, nearest.
Præ, before; *prĭor*, before; *prīmus*, first.

And some have no positive at all to which we can refer them; as,

detĕrior, worse; *detĕrrimus*, worst.
ōcyor, swifter; *ōcyssimus*, swiftest.
pŏtior, more desirable; *pŏtissimus*, most desirable.

Adjectives ending in *er* form the superlative degree from the nominative case, by adding *rĭmus*; as, of *pulcher* fair, *pulcher-rĭmus* fairest, or, most fair.

So too *vĕtus*, making in the gen. *vĕtĕris*, though it has no comparative, makes in the superlative *vĕterrĭmus*.

The following adjectives in *lis* change *is* into *līmus*:

Agĭl-is,   nimble;   *ăgil-līmus,*   nimblest,   or, most nimble.
Făcĭl-is,   easy;   *făcil-līmus,*   easiest,   or, most easy.
Grăcĭl-is,   slender;   *grăcil-līmus,*   slenderest,   or, most slender.
Hŭmĭl-is,   low;   *hŭmil-līmus,*   lowest,   or, most low.
Sĭmĭl-is,   like;   *sĭmil-līmus,*   likest,   or, most like.

Also, If a vowel comes before *us* in the nominative case of an adjective, the comparison is usually made by *măgis* more, and *maxĭmè* most; as,
Pius, godly; *măgis pius,* more godly; *maxĭmè pius,* most godly.*

OF A PRONOUN.

A *Pronoun* is a word used instead of a substantive, and is either itself a substantive, and called a *personal pronoun;* or an adjective, being either a *demonstrative,* or *relative,* or *interrogative* pronoun. There are also *possessive* pronouns, which are adjectives derived from the genitive cases of the personal pronouns.

The pronouns are:

Egŏ, I,   } The personal   *meus,* mine,   } Possessive pronouns.
tu, you,   } pronouns: *tuus,* your,   }
sui, of himself, }   *suus,* his own, }
                                  noster, ours,   }
                                  vester, yours, of *ye,* }

hic, this,   }   *qui,* who, the relative pro-
is, he,   }   noun, and its compounds
ille, he,   } Demon-   *quicunque, quisquis,* etc.
ipse, oneself,   } strative   *qui* or *quis,* who? the in-
idem, { (which is a } pronouns: terrogative pronoun.
        { compound of }
        { *is*) the same, }

The syllable *met,* giving additional emphasis to the pronoun, is often added to *ĕgŏ,* in all cases except the genitive, and to some of the cases of *tu* and of *sui;* but to the nominative of *tu, met* is not added, but *te,* as nom. *tūtĕ,* acc. *tūtĕmet.* The accusative and ablative cases of *sui* admit of a reduplication, as *sēsē.*

---

* Juvenal uses *egregiùs* as the comparative of the adverb *egregiè,* and *piissimus* occurs in Seneca; but these examples are not to be imitated.

DECLENSION OF PRONOUNS.

Ego, tu, sui, are pronouns substantive, and are thus declined:

	Singular.			Plural.	
N.	Ego,	I,	N.	Nos,	we,
G.	Mei,	of me,	G.	Nostr-ûm,	*vel* -i, of us,
D.	Mihi,*	to me,	D.	Nōbis,	to us,
A.	Me,	me,	A.	Nos,	us,
V.	—		V.	—	
A.	Me,	from, or, by me.	A.	Nōbis,	from, or, by us.

	Singular.			Plural.	
N.	Tu,	thou, or, you,	N.	Vos,	ye, or, you, [you,
G.	Tui,	of thee, or, you,	G.	Vestr-ûm,	*vel* -i, of ye, or,
D.	Tibi,	to thee, or, you,	D.	Vōbis,	to ye, or, you,
A.	Te,	thee, or, you,	A.	Vos,	ye, or, you,
V.	Tu,	o thou, or, you,	V.	Vos,	o ye,
A.	Te,	with thee, or, you.	A.	Vōbis,	with ye, or, you.

Sui,† of himself, herself, themselves, itself, has no nominative or vocative case, and is thus declined:

Singular and Plural.

G. Sui, of himself, ⎫
D. Sibi, to himself, ⎬ herself, themselves, &c.
A. Se, himself, ⎪
A. Se, by himself, ⎭

	Singular.				Plural.		
	M.	F.	N.		M.	F.	N.
N.	Hic,‡	hæc,	hoc,	N.	Ili,	hæ,	hæc,
G.	Hujus,			G.	Hōrum,	hărum,	hōrum,
D.	Huic,			D.	IIis,		
A.	Hunc,	hanc,	hoc,	A.	Hos,	has,	hæc,
V.	—			V.	—		
A.	Hôc,	hâc,	hôc.	A.	His.		

---

* In poetry often contracted into *mi*.

† *Sui* and its possessive *suus* are called *reflective* pronouns, because they refer to that person or thing which is the principal word in the sentence.

‡ To *hic* is often added *ce*, giving additional emphasis in all cases and genders; and in interrogative sentences, sometimes *cine* is added; as, *hujusce, hunccine, hosce,* etc.

Ille he, fem. *illa* she, neut. *illud* that, is thus declined:

	Singular.			Plural.	
M.	F.	N.	M.	F.	N.
N. Ille,	ill-a,	ill-ud,	N. Ill-i,	ill-æ,	ill-a,
G. Ill-ius,			G. Ill-ōrum,	ill-ārum,	ill-ōrum,
D. Ill-i,			D. Ill-is,		
A. Ill-um,	ill-am,	ill-ud,	A. Ill-os,	ill-as,	ill-a,
V. —			V. —		
A. Ill-o,	ill-â,	ill-o.	A. Ill-is.		

In like manner is also declined *iste* that, and *ipse* he himself; except that this last makes *ipsum* in the nominative and accusative cases singular of the neuter gender.

Is, ea, id, he, she, *or* that, is thus declined:

	Singular.			Plural.	
M.	F.	N.	M.	F.	N.
N. Is,	ea,	id,	N. Ii,	eæ,	ea,
G. Ejus,			G. Eórum,	eárum,	eórum,
D. Ei,			D. Iis, *vel,*	eis,	
A. Eum,	eam,	id,	A. Eos,	eas,	ea,
V. —			V. —		
A. Eo,	eâ,	eo.	A. Iis, *vel,*	eis.	

In like manner also is declined its compound, *idem* the same; as, nom. *ĭdem, eădem, ĭdem;* gen. *ejusdem,* &c.

The relative *qui,* who, is thus declined:

	Singular.			Plural.	
M.	F.	N.	M.	F.	N.
N. Qui,	quæ,	quod,	N. Qui,	quæ,	quæ,
G. Cujus,			G. Quorum,	quarum,	quorum,
D. Cui,			D. Quibus,*		
A. Quem,	quam,	quod,	A. Quos,	quas,	quæ,
V. —			V. —		
A. Quo,	quâ,	quo.	A. Quibus.		

In like manner also are declined its compounds, *quidam,* a certain one; *quivis, quilĭbet,* any one; *quicunque,* whosoever, &c. &c.

---

* *Quĭbus* is often contracted into *queis,* or *quis,* in poetry, and in some (but not in the purest) prose writers.

The *indefinite* pronoun *quis*, any one, (not found except after *si, nisi, num, ne, quo, quanto,* or *quum,*) is declined like *qui*, except that in the nom. sing. fem. and also in the nom. and acc. pl. neut. it makes both *quæ* and (more usually) *quă;* and in the nom. and acc. neut. sing. it makes *quid.*

The *interrogative* pronoun, when joined with a substantive, is *qui?** when standing without a substantive, the nom. sing. masc. is *quis?* and in the nom. and acc. sing. neut. *quid?*

Quisquis, whosoever, is confined to the following cases:

Nom. Quisquis, ——— quidquid, *or* quicquid,
Acc. ——— ——— quidquid, *or* quicquid,
Abl. M. Quoquo, N. quoquo.

OF A VERB.

A VERB is that part of speech by which it is declared that the subject of a sentence *does* or *suffers* something.

Verbs have two voices; the *active*, ending in *o;* the *passive*, ending in *or.*

Of verbs ending in *o* some are *transitive,* that is to say, in them the action passes on to a noun following; as, *amo te,* "I love you." And these verbs have a passive voice, which is made by changing *o* into *or;* as, *amor,* "I am loved."

Some are *intransitive,* that is to say, the action expressed by them does not pass on to any noun following, but is complete in itself; as, *curro,* "I run:" and these verbs have no passive voice.†

Three verbs, *fīo,* "I become;" *vāpŭlo,* "I am beaten;" *vēneo,* "I am sold," have a passive signification, but an active form (except that *fīo* makes *factus sum* in the perfect;) and are called *neutral passives.*

---

* There are a few instances of *quis* also being used with a substantive, but, except in poetry, it is seldom done, except to avoid an open vowel

† But, from these verbs, impersonal verbs are often formed of the third singular passive; as, *vīvĭtur,* "it is lived by men," that is to say, "men live, one lives," &c.; *ĭtur,* "men go, one goes," &c.; *ventum est,* "I, or you, or he came," &c.

Four verbs, *audeo,* "I dare;" *fido,* "I trust;" *gaudeo,* "I am glad;" and *soleo,* "I am accustomed," have the passive form with an active signification in the participle of the perfect tense, and in the tenses formed from it; as, *ausus sum,* &c. and these are called *neuter passives.*

Of verbs ending in *or* some are *passive,* as has been said above, and some are *deponent* verbs, being of a passive form (with the addition of gerunds and supines,) but of an active signification; some being *transitive;* as, *věněror Deum,* "I worship God;" and some *intransitive;* as, *mŏrior,* "I die."

Some verbs are used only in the third person singular, having no nominative case; as, *tŏnat,* "it thunders;" *ŏportet me,* "it behoves me;" and these are called verbs *impersonal.*

OF MOODS.

There are four moods, the indicative, imperative, subjunctive, and the infinitive.

The *indicative* mood either declares a thing positively; as, *ego amo,* "I do love;" or asks a question; as, *amas tu,* "dost thou love?"

The *imperative* mood expresses a command, a request, a wish, or an exhortation; as, *věni huc,* "come hither;" *parce mihi,* "spare me." It is also known by the sign *let;* as, *īto,* "let him go."*

The *subjunctive* or *potential* mood speaks of the subject as it is conceived in the mind; and is called *subjunctive,* when it is subjoined to another word or clause going before it; as, *nescio qualis sit,* "I know not what sort of man he is." It is called *potential,* when it signifies *power, duty, likelihood, inclination,* or *wish;* and in the second and third persons of the present and perfect it is sometimes used nearly in the sense of the impera-

---

* In grammars the imperative is usually given as consisting but of one tense; but the forms in *to* (active) and in *tor* (passive) have a more future sense than the other forms.

C

tive; as, *sis bŏnus,* "may you be propitious;" *ămet,* " let him love."

The *infinitive* mood has neither number, person, or nominative case before it; and is known commonly by the sign *to;* as, *amāre,* "to love." It is also often used as a nominative or accusative case neuter; as, *errāre humānum est,* " to err is human."

OF TENSES.

Verbs have six tenses or times, expressing the time of an action ; the present, the imperfect, the perfect, the pluperfect, and the first future, and second future, or future perfect.

The *present* tense speaks of a thing now existing, or now doing; as, *ămo,* " I love;" *lŏquor,* "I am speaking;" *sum,* " I am."

The *imperfect* tense speaks of a thing that was being done, but was not terminated, at some particular past time ; as, *ămābam,* " I was loving." And sometimes it expresses a habit ; as, *dīcēbam,* " I used to say." And is formed by changing—

    In the first conjugation *o* into *-ābam,*
    In the second . . *o* into *-bam,*
    In the third and fourth *o* into *-ēbam.**

The *perfect* tense speaks of an action terminated ; as, *ămāvi,* " I loved," or " have loved," and is formed as will be shewn in the *As in præsenti.*

The *pluperfect* speaks of a thing done at some time past, and then ended ; as, *ămāvĕram,* " I had loved;" and is formed from the perfect, by changing *i* into *ĕram.*

The *first future* tense speaks of a thing to be done hereafter; as, *ămābo,* " I shall love;" and is formed from the present by changing—

    In the first conjugation *o* into *ābo,*
    In the second . . *o* into *bo,*
    In the third and fourth *o* into *am.*

---

* The Poets often make the imperfect of the fourth conjugation in *-ibam,* instead of *-iebam;* as, "*Lenibat* dictis animum." Virg.

The *second future*, or *future perfect*, speaks of a thing which will have been done when something else has been done; as, *ămāvĕro*, "I shall have loved;" and is formed from the perfect, by changing *i* into *ĕro*.

GERUNDS AND SUPINES.

VERBS have three *gerunds*, ending in *di*, *do*, *dum*, which supply the oblique cases of the infinitive present active as, *ămandi*, "of loving;" *ămandum*, "loving;" *ămando*, "by loving," &c.; and they are formed from the present by changing—

In the first conjugation   *o* into *andi*,
In the second   . . *eo* into *endi*,
In the third and fourth   *o* into *endi*.

They have two *supines*, which are also used to supply cases for the infinitive and are formed, as will be taught in the *As in præsenti*.

The supine in *um* is used only with verbs expressing or implying a motion to a place; as, *eo dormītum*, "I go to sleep."

The supine in *u* has a passive sense, and is used only after adjectives, or after one or two substantives used as adjectives; as, *turpe factu*, "base to be done;" *nĕfas dictu*, "wicked to be said." But there are many verbs which have no supine.

PARTICIPLES.

THERE are four participles; two active, and two passive:—

The participle of the present active, which signifies a present action, and ends in *ans* in the first conjugation, and in *ens* in the others; as, *ămans*, "loving;" *mŏnens*, "warning."

The participle future active ending in *ūrus*, which signifies a likelihood or design of doing anything; as, *ămātūrus*, "about to love," or "likely to love."

c 2

The participle perfect passive, which signifies what is actually done and completed; as, *ămātus*, " loved ;" *mŏnĭtus*, " having been warned." But in deponent verbs this participle has commonly an active signification; as, *lŏcūtus hæc*, " having spoken these things."

Another participle passive, called also the *gerundive*, which denotes that what is spoken of must happen, ought to happen, or (sometimes) is actually happening, with respect to a person or thing; as, *ămandus*, " who must, or ought to be loved ;" *in ĕpistolā scribendā*, " in writing the letter."

OF NUMBERS AND PERSONS.

VERBS have two numbers, singular and plural, like nouns; and three persons in each number.

Singular.		Plural.	
1. Ego amo,	I love.	Nos amāmus,	We love.
2. Tu amas,	you love.	Vos amātis,	ye love.
3. Ille amat,	he loves.	Illi amant,	they love.

All nouns, except *ego* and *tu*, are of the third person.

OF THE VERB *Esse*, to be.

Before other verbs are declined, it is necessary to learn the verb esse, *to be.*

Sum, es, fui, esse, fŭtūrus, to be.

INDICATIVE MOOD.

1. Present Tense.—*am.*

Sing. Sum,	I am.	Plur. Sŭmus,	We are.
Ĕs,	you are.	Estis,	ye are.
Est,	he is.	Sunt,	they are.

2. Imperfect Tense.—*was.*

Sing. Ĕram,	I was.	Plur. Ĕrāmus,	We were.
Ĕras,	you were.	Ĕrātis,	ye were.
Ĕrat,	he was.	Ĕrant,	they were.

3. Perfect Tense.—*have.*

Sing. Fui,   *I have been.*
      Fuisti,   *you have been.*
      Fuit,   *he has been.*
Plur. Fuĭmus,   *We have been.*
      Fuistis,   *ye have been.*
      Fuĕrunt, *vel* fuēre,   *they have been.*

4. Pluperfect Tense.—*had.*

Sing. Fuĕram,   *I had been.*
      Fuĕras,   *you had been.*
      Fuĕrat,   *he had been.*
Plur. Fuĕrāmus,   *We had been.*
      Fuĕrātis,   *ye had been.*
      Fuĕrant,   *they had been.*

5. First Future Tense.—*shall,* or, *will.*

Sing. Ĕro,   *I shall be.*
      Ĕris,   *you will be.*
      Ĕrit,   *he will be.*
Plur. Ĕrĭmus,   *We shall be.*
      Ĕrĭtis,   *ye will be.*
      Ĕrunt,   *they will be.*

6. Second Future, or Future Perfect.—*shall have.*

Sing. Fuĕro,   *I shall have been,*
      Fuĕris,   *you will have been.*
      Fuĕrit,   *he will have been.*
Plur. Fuĕrĭmus,   *We shall have been.*
      Fuĕrītis,   *ye will have been.*
      Fuĕrint,   *they will have been.*

IMPERATIVE MOOD.

Sing. Es, esto,   *Be thou.*
      Esto,   *be he,* or, *let him be.*
Plur. Este, estōte,   *Be ye.*
      Sunto,   *be they,* or, *let them be.*

SUBJUNCTIVE, OR POTENTIAL MOOD.

1. Present Tense.—*may.*

Sing. Sim,   *I may be.*   Plur. Sīmus,   *We may be.*
       Sis,   *you may be.*   Sītis,   *ye may be.*
       Sit,   *he may be.*   Sint,   *they may be.*

2. Imperfect Tense.—*might,* &c.

Sing. Essem, *vel,* fŏrem,   *I might be.*
       Esses, *vel,* fŏres,   *you might be.*
       Esset, *vel,* fŏret,   *he might be.*
Plur. Essēmus, *vel,* fŏrēmus,   *We might be.*
       Essētis, *vel,* fŏrētis,   *ye might be.*
       Essent, *vel,* fŏrent,   *they might be.*

3. Perfect Tense.—*may have,* &c.

Sing. Fuĕrim,   *I may have been.*
       Fuĕris,   *you may have been.*
       Fuĕrit,   *he may have been.*
Plur. Fuĕrĭmus,   *We may have been.*
       Fuĕrĭtis,   *ye may have been.*
       Fuĕrint,   *they may have been.*

4. Pluperfect Tense.—*might, would have,* &c.

Sing. Fuissem,   *I might, or, would have been.*
       Fuisses,   *you might, or, would have been.*
       Fuisset,   *he might, or, would have been.*
Plur. Fuissēmus,   *We might, or, would have been.*
       Fuissētis,   *ye might, or, would have been.*
       Fuissent,   *they might, or, would have been.*

5. Future Tense.—*may be about,* &c.

Sing. Fŭtūrus sim,*   *I may be about to be.*
       Fŭtūrus sis,   *you may be about to be.*
       Fŭtūrus sit,   *he may be about to be.*
Plur. Fŭtūri sīmus,   *We may be about to be.*
       Fŭtūri sītis,   *ye may be about to be.*
       Fŭtūri sint,   *they may be about to be.*

---

* *Futūrus,* being in reality a participle, agrees with its substantive

INFINITIVE MOOD.

Present Tense,
Esse,   to be.

Perfect, and Pluperfect Tense,
Fuisse,   to have been.

Future Tense,
Fŏre, vel, Fŭtūrum esse,   to be about to be.

Participle future,*
Fŭtūrus,   about to be.

DECLENSION OF VERBS REGULAR.

VERBS have four conjugations, both in the active and passive voice.

The first conjugation has *ā* in the penultima (or last syllable but one) of the infinitive mood active; as, *ămo, ămāre*.†

The second has *ē;* as, *mŏnĕo, mŏnēre*.

The third has *ĕ;* as, *rĕgo, rĕgĕre*.

The fourth has *ī;* as, *audĭo, audīre*.

VERBS ACTIVE in *O* are declined after these examples.

1. Am-o, am-as, am-āvi, am-āre; aman-di, aman-do, amau-dum; amāt-um, amāt-u; am-ans, amātu-rus:
                                 to love.

---

in gender and number; so that in the singular it may be either *futurus, futura,* or *futurum;* in the plural, *futuri, -æ,* or *-a.*

* Some compounds of *sum* have also a present participle; as, *absum* to be absent, part. *absens,* absent, or being absent.

† Except *do,* " to give;" which makes *dăre, dătum*.

2. Mŏn-eo, mon-es, mon-ui, mon-ēre; monen-di, monen-do, monen-dum; monĭt-um, monĭt-u; mon-ens, monĭtū-rus: *to advise.*

3. Rĕg-o,* reg-is, rex-i, reg-ĕre; regen-di, regen-do, regen-dum; rect-um, rect-u; reg-ens, rectu-rus: *to rule.*

4. Aud-io, aud-is, aud-īvi, aud-īre; audien-di, audien-do, audien-dum; audīt-um, audīt-u; audi-ens, auditu-rus: *to hear.*

FIRST CONJUGATION.—*Amo.*
INDICATIVE MOOD.

1. Present Tense.—*do, am.*

Sing. Ăm-o,   *I love, am loving, or, do love.*
     ăm-as,   *you love, are loving, or, do love.*
     ăm-at,   *he loves, is loving, or, does love.*
Plur. Ăm-āmus,   *We love, are loving, or, do love.*
     ăm-ātis,   *ye love, are loving, or, do love.*
     ăm-ant,   *they love, are loving, or, do love.*

2. Imperfect Tense.—*did, was.*

Sing. Ăm-ābam,   *I did love, or, was loving.*
     am-ābas,   *you did love, or, were loving.*
     am-ābat,   *he did love, or, was loving.*
Plur. Am-ābāmus,   *We did love, or, were loving.*
     am-ābātis,   *ye did love, or, were loving.*
     am-ābant,   *they did love, or, were loving.*

3. Perfect Tense.—*have.*

Sing. Ămāv-i,   *I loved, or, have loved.*
     amāv-isti,   *you loved, or, have loved.*
     amāv-it,   *he loved, or, has loved.*
Plur. Amāv-ĭmus,   *We loved, or, have loved.*
     amāv-istis, *ye loved, or, have loved.*
     amāv-ērunt, *vel*-ēre, *they loved, or, have loved.*

---

* The following is the way in which a Verb of the third Conjugation ending in -*io* is declined:—Fŭg-io, fug-is, fūg-i, fug-ĕrĕ; fugien-di, fugien-do, fugien-dum; fugĭt-um, fugĭt-u; fugi-ens, fugĭtu-rus.

4. Pluperfect Tense.—*had.*

Sing. Ămāv-ĕram,   *I had loved.*
      amāv-ĕras,   *you had loved.*
      amāv-ĕrat,   *he had loved.*
Plur. Amāv-ĕrāmus,   *We had loved.*
      amāv-ĕrātis,   *ye had loved.*
      amāv-érant,   *they had loved.*

5. First Future Tense.—*shall,* or, *will.*

Sing. Ăm-ābo,   *I shall love.*
      am-ābis,   *you will love.*
      am-ābit,   *he will love.*
Plur. Am-ābĭmus,   *We shall love.*
      am-ābĭtis,   *ye will love.*
      am-ābunt,   *they will love.*

6. Second Future, or Future Perfect.—*shall have, will have.*

Sing. Ămāv-ĕro,   *I shall have loved.*
      amāv-ĕris,   *you will have loved.*
      amāv-ĕrit,   *he will have oved.*
Plur. Amāv-ĕrīmus,   *We shall have loved.*
      amāv-ĕrītis,   *ye will have loved.*
      amāv-ĕrint,   *they will have loved.*

IMPERATIVE MOOD.

Sing. Ăm-a, ăm-āto,   *Love thou.*
      am-āto,   *let him love.*
Plur. Am-āte, am-ātōte,   *Love ye.*
      am-anto,   *let them love.*

SUBJUNCTIVE, OR POTENTIAL MOOD.

1. Present Tense.—*may.*

Sing. Ăm-em,   *I may love.*
      am-es,   *you may love.*
      am-et,   *he may love.*
Plur. Am-ēmus,   *We may love.*
      am-ētis,   *ye may love.*
      am-ent,   *they may love.*

2. Imperfect Tense.—*might, should, would.*

Sing. Ăm-ārem,   *I might love.*
am-āres,   *you might love.*
am-āret,   *he might love.*
Plur. Am-ārēmus,   *We might love.*
am-ārētis,   *ye might love.*
am-ārent,   *they might love.*

3. Perfect Tense.—*may have.*

Sing. Ămāv-ĕrim,   *I may have loved.*
amāv-ĕris,   *you may have loved.*
amāv-ĕrit,   *he may have loved.*
Plur. Amāv-ĕrĭmus,   *We may have loved.*
amāv-ĕrĭtis,   *ye may have loved..*
amāv-ĕrint,   *they may have loved.*

4. Pluperfect Tense.—*would have, might have, could have*

Sing. Ămāv-issem,   *I would havè loved.*
amāv-isses,   *you would have loved.*
amāv-isset,   *he would have loved.*
Plur. Amāv-issēmus,   *We would have loved.*
amāv-issētis,   *ye would have loved.*
amāv-issent,   *they would have loved.*

5. Future Tense.—*may be about to.*

Sing. Ămātū-rus sim,   *I may be about to love.*
amatu-rus sis,   *you may be about to love.*
amatu-rus sit,   *he may be about to love.*
Plur. Amatu-ri simus,   *We may be about to love.*
amatu-ri sitis,   *ye may be about to love.*
amatu-ri sint,   *they may be about to love.*

INFINITIVE MOOD.
Present Tense.

Ămā-re,   *to love.*

Perfect, and Pluperfect Tense.

Ămāv-isse,   *to have loved.*

Future Tense.

Ămātū-rum esse, *or,* fŏre,   *to be about to love.*

GERUNDS.

Ăman-di,   *of loving.*
Aman-do,   *in loving.*
Aman-dum,   *to love.*

SUPINES.

Active,   Passive,
Ămāt-um, *to love.*   Ămāt-u, *to be loved.*

PARTICIPLES.

Present Tense,   Future,
Ăm-ans, *loving.*   Ămātū-rus, *about to love.*

~~~~~~~~~~~~~~~

SECOND CONJUGATION.—*Moneo.*

INDICATIVE MOOD.

1. Present Tense. —*do, am.*

Sing. Mŏn-eo,   *I advise, am advising,* or, *do advise.*
      mŏn-es,   *you advise, are advising* or, *do advise.*
      mŏn-et,   *he advises, is advising,* or, *does advise.*
Plur. Mŏn-ēmus,   *We advise, are advising,* or, *do advise.*
      mŏn-ētis,   *ye advise, are advising,* or, *do advise.*
      mŏn-ent,   *they advise, are advising,* or, *do advise.*

2. Imperfect Tense.—*did, was.*

Sing. Mŏn-ēbam,   *I did advise, or, was advising.*
      mŏn-ēbas,   *you did advise, or, were advising.*
      mŏn-ēbat,   *he did advise, or, was advising.*
Plur. Mŏn-ēbāmus,   *We did advise, or, were advising.*
      mŏn-ēbātis,   *ye did advise, or, were advising.*
      mŏn-ēbant,   *they did advise, or, were advising.*

3. Perfect Tense.—*have.*

Sing. Mŏnu-i,   *I advised, or, have advised.*
mŏnu-isti,   *you advised, or, have advised.*
mŏnu-it,   *he advised, or, has advised.*
Plur. Mŏnu-ĭmus,   *We advised, or, have advised.*
mŏnu-istis,   *ye advised, or, have advised.*
mŏnu-ērunt, *v.* -ēre, *they advised, or, have advised.*

4. Pluperfect Tense.—*had.*

Sing. Mŏnu-ĕram,   *I had advised.*
mŏnu-ĕras,   *you had advised.*
mŏnu-ĕrat,   *he had advised.*
Plur. Mŏnu-ĕrāmus,   *We had advised.*
mŏnu-ĕrātis,   *ye had advised.*
mŏnu-ĕrant,   *they had advised.*

5. First Future Tense.—*shall, or, will.*

Sing. Mŏnē-bo,   *I shall advise.*
mŏnē-bis,   *you will advise.*
mŏnē-bit,   *he will advise.*
Plur. Mŏnē-bĭmus,   *We shall, or, will advise.*
mŏnē-bĭtis,   *ye will advise.*
mŏnē-bunt,   *they will advise.*

6. Second Future, or Future Perfect Tense.—*shall have will have.*

Sing. Monu-ĕro,   *I shall have advised.*
monu-ĕris,   *you will have advised.*
monu-ĕrit,   *he will have advised.*
Plur. Monu-ĕrīmus,   *We shall have advised.*
monu-ĕrītis,   *ye will have advised.*
monu-ĕrint,   *they will have advised.*

IMPERATIVE MOOD.

Sing. Mŏn-e, mon-ēto,   *Advise thou.*
mon-ēto,   *let him advise.*
Plur. Mon-ēte, mon-ētōte,   *Advise ye.*
mon-ento,   *let them advise.*

SUBJUNCTIVE, OR POTENTIAL MOOD.

1. Present Tense.—*may.*

Sing. Mone-am,   *I may advise.*
       mone-as,   *you may advise.*
       mone-at,   *he may advise.*
Plur. Mone-āmus,   *We may advise.*
       mone-ātis,   *ye may advise.*
       mone-ant,   *they may advise.*

2. Imperfect Tense.—*might, would.*

Sing. Monē-rem,   *I might advise.*
       monē-res,   *you might advise.*
       monē-ret,   *he might advise.*
Plur. Monē-rēmus,   *We might advise.*
       monē-rētis,   *ye might advise.*
       monē-rent,   *they might advise.*

3. Perfect Tense.—*may have.*

Sing. Monu-ĕrim,   *I may have advised.*
       monu-ĕris,   *you may have advised.*
       monu-ĕrit,   *he may have advised.*
Plur. Monu-ĕrĭmus,   *We may have advised.*
       monu-ĕrĭtis,   *ye may have advised.*
       monu-ĕrint,   *they may have advised.*

4. Pluperfect Tense.—*would have, might have, could have.*

Sing. Monu-issem,   *I would have advised.*
       monu-isses,   *you would have advised.*
       monu-isset,   *he would have advised.*
Plur. Monu-issēmus,   *We would have advised.*
       monu-issētis,   *ye would have advised.*
       monu-issent,   *they would have advised.*

5. Future Tense.—*may be about to.*

Sing. Mŏnĭtū-rus sim,   *I may be about to advise.*
       monitu-rus sis,   *you may be about to advise.*
       monitu-rus sit,   *he may be about to advise.*
Plur. Mŏnĭtū-ri simus,   *We may be about to advise.*
       monitu-ri sītis,   *ye may be about to advise.*
       monitu-ri sint,   *they may be about to advise.*

INFINITIVE MOOD.

Present Tense.

Mon-ēre, to advise.

Perfect, and Pluperfect Tense.

Monu-isse, to have advised.

Future Tense.

Monĭtū-rum esse, *or* fŏre, to be about to advise.

GERUNDS.

Monen-di, of advising.
monen-do, in advising.
monen-dum, to advise.

SUPINES.

Active.   Passive.
Monĭt-um, *to advise.*   Monĭt-u, *to be advised.*

PARTICIPLES.

Present Tense.   Future.
Mon-ens, *advising.*   Monĭtū-rus, *about to advise.*

THIRD CONJUGATION.—Rĕgo.

INDICATIVE MOOD.

1. Present Tense.—*do, am.*

Sing. Rĕg-o,   *I rule, am ruling,* or, *do rule.*
rĕg-is,   *you rule, are ruling,* or, *do rule.*
rĕg-it,   *he rules, is ruling,* or, *does rule.*
Plur. Rĕg-ĭmus,   *We rule, are ruling,* or, *do rule.*
rĕg-ĭtis,   *ye rule, are ruling,* or, *do rule.*
rĕg-unt,   *they rule, are ruling,* or, *do rule.*

2. Imperfect Tense.—*did, was*..

Sing. Rĕgē-bam,   *I did rule, or, was ruling.*
rĕgē-bas,   *you did rule, or, were ruling.*
rĕgē-bat,   *he did rule, or, was ruling.*
Plur. Rĕgē-bāmus,   *We did rule, or, were ruling.*
rĕgē-bātis,   *ye did rule, or, were ruling,*
rĕgē-bant,   *they did rule, or, were ruling.*

3. Perfect Tense.—*have.*

Sing. Rex-i,   *I ruled, or, have ruled.*
rex-isti,   *you ruled, or, have ruled.*
rex-it,   *he ruled, or, has ruled.*
Plur. Rex-ĭmus,   *We ruled, or, have ruled.*
rex-istis,   *ye ruled, or, have ruled.*
rex-ērunt, *v.* ēre,   *they ruled, or, have ruled.*

4. Pluperfect Tense.—*had.*

Sing. Rex-ĕram,   *I had ruled.*
rex-ĕras,   *you had ruled.*
rex-ĕrat,   *he had ruled.*
Plur. Rex-ĕrāmus,   *We had ruled.*
rex-ĕrātis,   *ye had ruled.*
rex-ĕrant,   *they had ruled.*

5. First Future Tense.—*shall, or, will.*

Sing. Rĕg-am,   *I shall rule.*
rĕg-es,   *you will rule.*
rĕg-et,   *he will rule.*
Plur. Rĕg-ēmus,   *We shall rule.*
rĕg-ētis,   *ye shall rule.*
rĕg-ent,   *they will rule.*

6. Second Future, or, Future Perfect Tense.—*shall have, will have.*

Sing. Rex-ĕro,   *I shall have ruled.*
rex-ĕris,   *you will have ruled.*
rex-ĕrit,   *he will have ruled.*
Plur. Rex-ĕrīmus,   *We shall have ruled.*
rex-ĕrītis,   *ye will have ruled.*
rex-ĕrint,   *they will have ruled.*

IMPERATIVE MOOD.

Sing. Rĕg-e, reg-ĭto,   *Rule thou.*
      rĕg-ĭto,   *let him rule.*
Plur. Rĕg-ĭte, reg-ĭtote,   *Rule ye.*
      rĕg-unto,   *let them rule.*

SUBJUNCTIVE, OR POTENTIAL MOOD.

1. Present Tense.—*may.*

Sing. Rĕg-am,   *I may rule.*
      rĕg-as,   *you may rule.*
      rĕg-at,   *he may rule.*
Plur. Rĕg-āmus,   *We may rule.*
      rĕg-ātis,   *ye may rule.*
      rĕg-ant,   *they may rule.*

2. Imperfect Tense.—*might.*

Sing. Rĕg-ĕrem,   *I might rule.*
      rĕg-ĕres,   *you might rule.*
      rĕg-ĕret,   *he might rule.*
Plur. Rĕg-ĕrēmus,   *We might rule.*
      rĕg-ĕrētis,   *ye might rule.*
      rĕg-ĕrent,   *they might rule.*

3. Perfect Tense.—*may have.*

Sing. Rex-ĕrim,   *I may have ruled.*
      rex-ĕris,   *you may have ruled.*
      rex-ĕrit,   *he may have ruled.*
Plur. Rex-ĕrĭmus,   *We may have ruled.*
      rex-ĕrĭtis,   *ye may have ruled.*
      rex-ĕrint,   *they may have ruled.*

4. Pluperfect Tense.—*would have, might have, could have.*

Sing. Rex-issem,   *I would have ruled.*
      rex-isses,   *you would have ruled.*
      rex-isset,   *he would have ruled.*
Plur. Rex-issēmus,   *We would have ruled.*
      rex-issētis,   *ye would have ruled.*
      rex-issent,   *they would have ruled.*

5. Future Tense.—*may be about to.*

Sing. Rectū-rus sim,   *I may be about to rule.*
rectū-rus sis,   *you may be about to rule.*
rectū-rus sit,   *he may be about to rule.*
Plur. Rectū-ri sīmus,   *We may be about to rule.*
rectū-ri sītis,   *ye may be about to rule.*
rectū-ri sint,   *they may be about to rule.*

INFINITIVE MOOD.

Present Tense.
Reg-ĕre,   *to rule.*

Perfect, and Pluperfect Tense.
Rex-isse,   *to have ruled.*

Future Tense.
Rectū-rum esse, *or* fŏre,   *to be about to rule.*

GERUNDS.
Regen-di,   *of ruling.*
regen-do,   *in ruling.*
regen-dum,   *to rule.*

SUPINES.
Active.   Passive.
Rect-um, *to rule.*   Rect-u, *to be ruled.*

PARTICIPLES.
Present Tense.   Future.
Reg-ens, *ruling.*   Rectū-rus, *about to rule.*

FOURTH CONJUGATION.—Audio.
INDICATIVE MOOD.
1. Present Tense.—*do, am.*

Sing. Aud-io,   *I hear, am hearing,* or, *do hear.*
aud-is,   *you hear, are hearing,* or, *do hear.*
aud-it,   *he hears, is hearing,* or, *does hear.*
Plur. Aud-īmus,   *We hear, are hearing,* or, *do hear.*
aud-ītis,   *ye hear, are hearing,* or, *do hear.*
aud-iunt,   *they hear, are hearing,* or, *do hear.*

2. Imperfect Tense.—*did, was.*

Sing. Audiē-bam,   *I did hear, or, was hearing.*
audiē-bas,   *you did hear, or, were hearing.*
audiē-bat,   *he did hear, or, was hearing.*
Plur. Audiē-bāmus,   *We did hear, or, were hearing.*
audiē-bātis,   *ye did hear, or, were hearing.*
audiē-bant,   *they did hear, or, were hearing.*

3. Perfect Tense.—*have.*

Sing. Audīv-i,   *I heard, or, have heard.*
audīv-isti,   *you heard, or, have heard.*
audīv-it,   *he heard, or, has heard.*
Plur. Audīv-ĭmus,   *We heard, or, have heard.*
audīv-istis,   *ye heard, or, have heard.*
audīv-ērunt, *v.* -ēre, *they heard, or, have heard.*

4. Pluperfect Tense.—*had.*

Sing. Audīv-ĕram,   *I had heard.*
audīv-ĕras,   *you had heard.*
audīv-ĕrat,   *he had heard.*
Plur. Audīv-ĕrāmus,   *We had heard.*
audīv-ĕrātis,   *ye had heard.*
audīv-ĕrant,   *they had heard.*

5. First Future Tense.—*shall, or, will.*

Sing. Audi-am,   *I shall hear.*
audi-es,   *you will hear.*
audi-et,   *he will hear.*
Plur. Audi-ēmus,   *We shall hear.*
audi-ētis,   *ye will hear.*
audi-ent,   *they will hear.*

6. Second Future, or Future Perfect.—*shall have, will have.*

Sing. Audīv-ĕro,   *I shall have heard.*
Audīv-ĕris,   *you will have heard.*
Audīv-ĕrit,   *he will have heard.*
Plur. Audīv-ĕrĭmus,   *We shall have heard.*
Audīv-ĕrītis,   *ye will have heard.*
Audīv-ĕrint,   *they will have heard.*

IMPERATIVE MOOD.

Sing. Aud-ĭ, aud-īto,   *Hear thou,*
       aud-īto,   *let him hear.*
Plur. Aud-īte, aud-ītōte,   *Hear ye.*
       aud-iŭnto,   *let them hear.*

SUBJUNCTIVE, OR POTENTIAL MOOD.

1. Present Tense.—*may.*

Sing. Audi-am,   *I may hear.*
      audi-as,   *you may hear.*
      audi-at,   *he may hear.*
Plur. Audi-āmus,   *We may hear.*
      audi-ātis,   *ye may hear.*
      audi-ant,   *they may hear.*

2. Imperfect Tense.—*might.*

Sing. Audī-rem,   *I might hear.*
      audī-res,   *you might hear.*
      audī-ret,   *he might hear.*
Plur. Audī-rēmus,   *We might hear.*
      audī-rētis,   *ye might hear.*
      audī-rent,   *they might hear.*

3. Perfect Tense.—*may have.*

Sing. Audīv-ĕrim,   *I may have heard.*
      audīv-ĕris,   *you may have heard.*
      audīv-ĕrit,   *he may have heard.*
Plur. Audīv-ĕrĭmus,   *We may have heard.*
      audīv-ĕrĭtis,   *ye may have heard.*
      audīv-ĕrint,   *they may have heard.*

4. Pluperfect Tense.—*would have, might have, could have.*

Sing. Audīv-issem,   *I would have heard.*
      audīv-isses,   *you would have heard.*
      audīv-isset,   *he would have heard.*
Plur. Audīv-issēmus,   *We would have heard.*
      audīv-issētis,   *ye would have heard.*
      audīv-issent,   *they would have heard.*

5. Future Tense.—*may be about to.*

Sing. Audītū-rus sim,   *I may be about to hear.*
audītū-rus sis,   *you may be about to hear.*
audītū-rus sit,   *he may be about to hear.*
Plur. Audītū-ri sīmus,   *We may be about to hear.*
audītū-ri sītis,   *ye may be about to hear.*
audītū-ri sint,   *they may be about to hear.*

INFINITIVE MOOD.
Present Tense.

Aud-īre,   *to hear.*

Perfect, and Pluperfect Tense.

Audīv-isse,   *to have heard.*

Future Tense.

Audītū-rum esse, *or* fŏre,   *to be about to hear.*

GERUNDS.

Audien-di,   *of hearing.*
audien-do,   *in hearing.*
audien-dum,   *to hear.*

SUPINES.

Active.   Passive.
Audīt-um, *to hear.*   Audīt-u, *to be heard.*

PARTICIPLES.

Present Tense.   Future.
Audi-ens, *hearing.*   Audītū-rus, *about to hear.*

IMPERSONAL VERBS are conjugated thus:
Present.

Sing. Děcet me,   It becomes me, or, I ought.
      děcet te,   it becomes you, or, you ought.
      děcet illum,   it becomes him, or, he ought.
Plur. Děcet nos,   It becomes us, or, we ought.
      děcet vos,   it becomes you, or, ye ought.
      děcet illos,   it becomes them, or, they ought.

Imperfect.
Děcēbat me,
děcēbat te, &c.

Like the third sing. of *moneo*; and so on, through all the tenses.

DECLENSION OF VERBS PASSIVE.

VERBS PASSIVE in *OR* are thus declined:

1. Ăm-or, ăm-āris *vel* am-āre, amāt-us sum *vel** fui; am-āri; amāt-us, aman-dus;   *to be loved.*
2. Mŏn-ēor, mon-ēris *vel* mon-ēre, mŏnĭt-us sum *vel* fui; mon-ēri; monit-us, monén-dus;   *to be advised.*
3. Rĕg-or, rĕg-ĕris *vel* reg-ĕre, rect-us sum *vel* fui; reg-i; rectus, regén-dus;   *to be ruled.*
4. Aud-ior, aud-īris *vel* aud-īre, audīt-us sum *vel* fui; aud-īri; audīt-us, audién-dus;   *to be heard.*

FIRST CONJUGATION.—Amor.
INDICATIVE MOOD.
1. Present Tense.—*am.*

Sing. Ămor,   *I am loved.*
     amāris, *v.* am-āre,   *you are loved.*
     am-ātur,   *he is loved.*
Plur. Am-āmur,   *We are loved.*
     am-āmĭni,   *ye are loved.*
     am-antur,   *they are loved.*

---

* There are, however, very few instances (if any) of such forms as *amatus fui* being used, by good authors, as the perfect tense, and equivalent to *amatus sum.*

2. Imperfect Tense.—*was, was being.*

Sing. Am-ābar,   *I was loved.*
       am-ābāris, *v.* -ābāre,   *you were loved.*
       am-ābātur,   *he was loved.*
Plur. Am-ābāmur,   *We were loved.*
       am-ābāmĭni,   *ye were loved.*
       am-ābantur,   *they were loved.*

3. Perfect Tense.—*was, have been.*

Sing. Amāt-us sum, *vel* fui,   *I have been loved.*
       amāt-us es, *v.* fuisti,   *you have been loved.*
       amāt-us est, *v.* fuit,   *he has been loved.*
Plur. Amāt-i sŭmus, *v.* fuĭmus, *We have been loved.*
       amāt-i estis, *v.* fuistis,   *ye have been loved.*
       amāt-i sunt, fuērunt, *v.*-ēre, *they have been loved.*

4. Pluperfect Tense.—*had been.*

Sing. Amāt-us ĕram, *v.* fuĕram, *I had been loved.*
       amāt-us ĕras, *v.* fuĕras,   *you had been loved.*
       amāt-us ĕrat, *v.* fuĕrat,   *he had been loved.*
Plur. Amāt-i ĕrāmus, *v.* fuĕrāmus, *We had been loved.*
       amat-i ĕrātis, *v.* fuĕrātis,   *ye had been loved.*
       amāt-i ĕrant, *v.* fuĕrant,   *they had been loved.*

5. First Future Tense.—*shall, or, will be.*

Sing. Am-ābor,   *I shall be loved.*
       am-ābĕris, *v.* -ābĕre,   *you will be loved.*
       am-ābĭtur,   *he will be loved.*
Plur. Am-ābĭmur,   *We shall be loved.*
       am-ābĭmini,   *ye will be loved.*
       am-ābuntur,   *they will be loved.*

6. Second Future, or Future Perfect.—*shall have been, will have been.*

Sing. Amāt-us ĕro, *v.* fuĕro,   *I shall have been loved.*
       amāt-us ĕris, *v.* fuĕris,   *you will have been loved.*
       amāt-us ĕrit, *v.* fuĕrit,   *he will have been loved.*
Plur. Amāt-i ĕrĭmus, *v.* fuĕrīmus, *We shall have been loved.*
       amāt-i ĕrĭtis, *v.* fuĕrītis,   *ye will have been loved.*
       amāt-i ĕrunt, *v.* fuĕrint,   *they will have been loved.*

IMPERATIVE MOOD.

Sing. Am-āre, am-ātor,   Be thou loved.
       am-ātor,   let him be loved.
Plur. Am-āmĭni, am-āmĭnor,   Be ye loved.
       am-antor,   let them be loved.

SUBJUNCTIVE, OR POTENTIAL MOOD.

1. Present Tense.—*may, can, would, should be.*

Sing. Am-er,   I may be loved.
       am-ēris, v. am-ēre,   you may be loved.
       am-ētur,   he may be loved.
Plur. Am-ēmur,   We may be loved.
       am-ēmĭni,   ye may be loved.
       am-entur,   they may be loved.

2. Imperfect Tense.—*might, should be.*

Sing. Am-ārer,   I might be loved.
       am-ārēris, v. -ārēre,   you might be loved.
       am-ārētur,   he might be loved.
Plur. Am-ārēmur,   We might be loved.
       am-ārēmini,   ye might be loved.
       am-ārentur,   they might be loved.

3. Perfect Tense.—*may have been.*

Sing. Amāt-us sim, v. fuerim,   I may have been loved.
       amāt-us sis, v. fueris,   you may have been loved.
       amāt-us sit, v. fuerit,   he may have been loved.
Plur. Amāt-i simus, v. fuerĭmus, We may have been loved.
       amāt-i sitis, v. fuerĭtis,   ye may have been loved.
       amāt-i sint, v. fuerint,   they may have been loved.

4. Pluperfect Tense.—*might, could, would have been.*

Sing. Amāt-us essem, v. fuissem, I would have been loved.
       amāt-us esses, v. fuisses,   you would have been loved.
       amāt-us esset, v. fuisset,   he would have been loved.
Plur. Amāt-i essēmus,v.fuissēmus, We would have been loved.
       amāt-i essētis, v. fuissētis, ye would have been loved.
       amāt-i essent, v. fuissent, they would have been loved.

INFINITIVE MOOD.

Present Tense.

Am-āri,   to be loved.

Perfect, and Pluperfect Tense.

Amāt-um esse, *vel* fuisse,   to have been loved.

Future Tense.

Amāt-um iri,   to be about to be loved.

PARTICIPLES.

The Perfect Tense.

Amāt-us,   loved, or, being loved.

The Participle in *dus*, or gerundive.
Aman-dus,   to be loved.

SECOND CONJUGATION.—Moneor.

INDICATIVE MOOD.

1. Present Tense.—*am*.

Sing. Mŏn-eor,   I am advised.
mon-ēris, *v.* -ēre,   you are advised.
mon-ētur,   he is advised.
Plur. Mon-ēmur,   We are advised.
mon-ēmĭni,   ye are advised.
mon-entur,   they are advised.

2. Imperfect Tense.—*was, was being.*

Sing. Mon-ēbar,   I was advised.
mon-ēbāris, *v.* -ēbāre,   you were advised.
mon-ēbātur,   he was advised.
Plur. Mon-ēbāmur,   We were advised.
mon-ēbāmĭni,   ye were advised.
mon-ēbantur,   they were advised.

3. Perfect Tense.—*was, have been.*

Sing. Monĭt-us sum, *v.* fui,   *I have been advised.*
monĭt-us es, *v.* fuisti,   *you have been advised.*
monĭt-us est, *v.* fuit,   *he has been advised.*
Plur. Monĭt-i sumus, *v.* fuĭmus,   *We have been advised.*
monĭt-i estis, *v.* fuistis,   *ye have been advised.*
monĭt-i sunt,fuērunt,*v.*fuēre,*they have been advised.*

4. Pluperfect Tense.—*had been.*

Sing. Monĭt-us ĕram, *v.* fuĕram,   *I had been advised.*
monĭt-us ĕras, *v.* fuĕras,   *you had been advised.*
monĭt-us ĕrat, *v.* fuĕrat,   *he had been advised.*
Plur. Monĭt-i ĕrāmus,*v.*fuĕrāmus, *We had been advised.*
monĭt-i ĕrātis, *v.* fuĕrātis,   *ye had been advised.*
monĭt-i ĕrant, *v.* fuĕrant,   *they had been advised.*

5. First Future Tense.—*shall, or, will be.*

Sing. Mon-ēbor,   *I shall be advised.*
mon-ebĕris, *v.* ēbĕre,   *you will be advised.*
mon-ēbĭtur,   *he will be advised.*
Plur. Mon-ēbĭmur,   *We shall be advised.*
mon-ēbĭmĭni,   *ye will be advised.*
mon-ēbuntur,   *they will be advised.*

6. Second Future, or Future Perfect Tense.—*shall have been, will have been.*

Sing. Monĭt-us ĕro, *v.* fuĕro,   *I shall have been advised.*
monĭt-us ĕris, *v.* fuĕris,   *you will have been advised.*
monĭt-us ĕrit, *v.* fuĕrit,   *he will have been advised.*
Plur. Monĭt-i ĕrĭmus,*v.*fuĕrĭmus,*We shall have been advised.*
monĭt-i ĕrĭtis, *v.* fuĕrītis, *ye will have been advised.*
monĭt-i ĕrunt, *v.* fuĕrint,   *they will have been advised.*

IMPERATIVE MOOD.

Sing. Mon-ēre, mon-ētor,   *Be thou advised.*
mon-ētor,   *let him be advised.*
Plur. Mon-ēmĭni, mon-ēmĭnor,*Be ye advised.*
mon-entor,   *let them be advised.*

SUBJUNCTIVE, OR POTENTIAL MOOD.

1. Present Tense.—*may, can, would, should be.*

Sing. Mon-ear,   *I may be advised.*
mon-eāris, *v.* mon-eāre,   *you may be advised.*
mon-eātur,   *he may be advised.*
Plur. Mon-eāmur,   *We may be advised.*
mon-eāmĭni,   *ye may be advised.*
mon-eantur,   *they may be advised.*

2. Imperfect Tense.—*might, should be.*

Sing. Mon-ērer,   *I might be advised.*
mon-ērēris, *v.* -ērēre,   *you might be advised.*
mon-ērētur,   *he might be advised.*
Plur. Mon-ērēmur,   *We might be advised.*
mon-ērēmĭni,   *ye might be advised.*
mon-ērentur,   *they might be advised.*

3. Perfect Tense.—*may have been.*

Sing. Monĭt-us sim, *v.* fuĕrim,   *I may have been advised.*
monĭt-us sis, *v.* fuĕris,   *you may have been advised.*
monĭt-us sit, *v.* fuĕrit,   *he may have been advised.*
Plur. Monĭt-i sīmus, *v.* fuĕrĭmus, *We may have been advised.*
monĭt-i sītis, *v.* fuĕrĭtis,   *ye may have been advised.*
monĭt-i sint, *v.* fuĕrint,   *they may have been advised.*

4. Pluperfect Tense.—*might, could, would have been.*

Sing. Monĭt-us essem, *v.* fuissem,   *I would have been advised.*
monĭt-us esses, *v.* fuisses,   *you would have been advised.*
monĭt-us esset, *v.* fuisset,   *he would have been advised.*
Plur. Monĭt-i essēmus, *v.* fuissēmus, *We would have been advised.*
monĭt-i essētis, *v.* fuissētis,   *ye would have been advised.*
monĭt-i essent, *v.* fuissent,   *they would have been advised.*

INFINITIVE MOOD.

Present Tense.

Mon-ēri,   *to be advised.*

Perfect and Pluperfect Tense.
Monĭt-um esse, *vel* fuisse,   *to have been advised.*

Future Tense.
Monĭt-um īri,   *to be about to be advised.*

PARTICIPLES.

The Perfect Tense.
Monĭt-us,   *advised, or, being advised.*

The Participle in *dus*, or the gerundive.
Monen-dus,   *to be advised.*

THIRD CONJUGATION.—Rĕgor.
INDICATIVE MOOD.
1. Present Tense.—*am.*

Sing. Rĕg-or,   *I am ruled.*
reg-ĕris, *v.* reg-ĕre,   *you are ruled.*
reg-ĭtur,   *he is ruled.*
Plur. Reg-ĭmur,   *We are ruled.*
reg-ĭmĭni,   *ye are ruled.*
reg-untur,   *they are ruled.*

2. Imperfect Tense.—*was, was being.*

Sing. Reg-ēbar,   *I was ruled.*
reg-ēbāris, *v.* ēbāre,   *you were ruled.*
reg-ēbātur,   *he was ruled.*
Plur. Reg-ēbāmur,   *We were ruled.*
reg-ēbāmĭni,   *ye were ruled.*
reg-ēbantur,   *they were ruled.*

3. Perfect Tense.—*was, have been.*

Sing. Rect-us sum, *v.* fui,   *I have been ruled.*
rect-us es, *v.* fuisti,   *you have been ruled.*
rect-us est, *v.* fuit,   *he has been ruled.*
Plur. Rect-i sŭmus, *v.* fuĭmus,   *We have been ruled.*
rect-i estis, *v.* fuistis,   *ye have been ruled.*
rect-i sunt, fuērunt, *v.* fuēre, *they have been ruled.*

4. Pluperfect Tense.—*had been.*

Sing. Rect-us ĕram, *v.* fuĕram,   *I had been ruled.*
       rect-us ĕras, *v.* fuĕras,   *you had been ruled.*
       rect-us ĕrat, *v.* fuĕrat,   *he had been ruled.*
Plur. Rect-i ĕrāmus, *v.* fuĕrāmus, *We had been ruled.*
       rect-i ĕrātis, *v.* fuĕrātis,   *ye had been ruled.*
       rect-i ĕrant, *v.* fuĕrant,   *they had been ruled.*

5. First Future Tense.—*shall,* or, *will be.*

Sing. Reg-ar,   *I shall be ruled.*
       reg-ēris, *v.* reg-ēre,   *you will be ruled.*
       reg-ētur,   *he will be ruled.*
Plur. Reg-ēmur,   *We shall be ruled.*
       reg-ēmĭni,   *ye will be ruled.*
       reg-entur,   *they will be ruled.*

6. Second Future, or Future Perfect Tense.—*shall have been, will have been.*

Sing. Rect-us ĕro, *v.* fuĕro,   *I shall have been ruled.*
       rect-us ĕris, *v.* fuĕris,   *you will have been ruled.*
       rect-us ĕrit, *v.* fuĕrit,   *he will have been ruled.*
Plur. Rect-i ĕrĭmus *v.* fuĕrĭmus, *We shall have been ruled.*
       rect-i ĕrĭtis, *v.* fuĕrĭtis,   *ye will have been ruled.*
       rect-i ĕrunt, *v.* fuĕrint,   *they will have been ruled.*

IMPERATIVE MOOD.

Sing. Rĕg-ĕre, reg-ĭtor,   *Be thou ruled.*
       reg-ĭtor,   *let him be ruled.*
Plur. Reg-ĭmĭni, reg-ĭmĭnor,   *Be ye ruled.*
       reg-untor,   *let them be ruled.*

SUBJUNCTIVE, OR POTENTIAL MOOD.

1. Present Tense.—*may, can, would, should be.*

Sing. Reg-ar,   *I may be ruled.*
       reg-āris, *v.* reg-āre,   *you may be ruled.*
       reg-ātur,   *he may be ruled.*
Plur. Reg-āmur,   *We may be ruled.*
       reg-āmĭni,   *ye may be ruled.*
       reg-antur,   *they may be ruled.*

2. Imperfect Tense.—*might, should be.*

Sing. Reg-ĕrer,   *I might be ruled.*
      reg-ĕrēris, *v.* reg-ĕrēre, *you might be ruled.*
      reg-ĕrētur,   *he might be ruled.*
Plur. Reg-ĕrēmur,   *We might be ruled.*
      reg-ĕrēmĭni,   *ye might be ruled.*
      reg-ĕrentur,   *they might be ruled.*

3. Perfect Tense.—*may have been.*

Sing. Rect-us sim, *v.* fuĕrim,   *I may have been ruled.*
      rect-us sis, *v.* fuĕris,   *you may have been ruled.*
      rect-us sit, *v.* fuĕrit,   *he may have been ruled.*
Plur. Rect-i sīmus, *v.* fuĕrĭmus,   *We may have been ruled.*
      rect-i sītis, *v.* fuĕrĭtis,   *ye may have been ruled.*
      rect-i sint, *v.* fuĕrint,   *they may have been ruled.*

4. Pluperfect Tense.—*might, could, would have been.*

Sing. Rect-us essem, *v.* fuissem,   *I would have been ruled.*
      rect-us esses, *v.* fuisses,   *you would have been ruled.*
      rect-us esset, *v.* fuisset,   *he would have been ruled.*
Plur. Rect-i essēmus, *v.* fuissēmus, *We would have been ruled.*
      rect-i essētis, *v.* fuissētis,   *ye would have been ruled.*
      rect-i essent, *v.* fuissent,   *they would have been ruled.*

INFINITIVE MOOD.

Present Tense.

Reg-i,   *to be ruled.*

Perfect and Pluperfect Tense.

Rect-um esse, *vel* fuisse,   *to have been ruled.*

Future Tense.

Rect-um īri,   *to be about to be ruled.*

PARTICIPLES.

The Perfect Tense.

Rect-us,   *ruled,* or, *being ruled.*

The Participle in *dus*, or gerundive.

Regen-dus,   *to be ruled.*

FOURTH CONJUGATION.—Audior.
INDICATIVE MOOD.

1. Present Tense.—*am.*

Sing. Aud-ior,   *I am heard.*
      aud-īris, *v.* aud-īre,   *you are heard.*
      aud-ītur,   *he is heard.*
Plur. Aud-īmur,   *We are heard.*
      aud-īmĭni,   *ye are heard.*
      aud-iuntur,   *they are heard.*

2. Imperfect Tense.—*was, was being.*

Sing. Aud-iēbar,   *I was heard.*
      aud-iēbāris, *v.* aud-iēbāre,   *you were heard.*
      aud-iēbătur,   *he was heard.*
Plur. Aud-iēbāmur,   *We were heard.*
      aud-iēbāmĭni,   *ye were heard.*
      aud-iēbantur,   *they were heard.*

3. Perfect Tense.—*was, have been.*

Sing. Audīt-us sum, *v.* fui,   *I have been heard.*
      audīt-us es, *v.* fuisti,   *you have been heard.*
      audīt-us est, *v.* fuit,   *he has been heard.*
Plur. Audīt-i sŭmus, *v.* fuĭmus,   *We have been heard.*
      audīt-i estis, *v.* fuistis,   *ye have been heard.*
      audīt-i sunt, fuĕrunt,*v.*fuēre,*they have been heard.*

4. Pluperfect Tense.—*had been.*

Sing. Audīt-us ĕram, *v.* fuĕram,   *I had been heard.*
      audīt-us ĕras, *v.* fuĕras,   *you had been heard.*
      audīt-us ĕrat, *v.* fuĕrat,   *he had been heard.*
Plur. Audīt-i ĕrāmus, *v.* fuĕrāmus,*We had been heard.*
      audīt-i ĕrātis, *v.* fuĕrātis,   *ye had been heard.*
      audīt-i ĕrant, *v.* fuĕrant,   *they had been heard.*

5. First Future Tense.—*shall, or, will be.*

Sing. Aud-iar,   *I shall be heard.*
      aud-iēris, *v.* aud-iēre,   *you will be heard.*
      aud-iētur,   *he will be heard.*
Plur. Aud-iēmur,   *We shall be heard.*
      aud-iēmĭni,   *ye will be heard.*
      aud-ientur,   *they will be heard.*

6. Second Future, or Future Perfect Tense.—*shall have been, will have been.*

Sing. Audīt-us ĕro, *v.* fuĕro,   *I shall have been heard.*
audīt-us ĕris, *v.* fuĕris,   *you will have been heard.*
audīt-us ĕrit, *v.* fuĕrit,   *he will have been heard.*
Plur. Audīt-i ĕrĭmus, *v.* fuĕrĭmus, *We shall have been heard.*
audīt-i ĕrĭtis, *v.* fuĕrītis,   *ye will have been heard.*
audīt-i ĕrunt, *v.* fuĕrint,   *they will have been heard.*

IMPERATIVE MOOD.

Sing. Aud-īre, aud-ītor,   *Be thou heard.*
audī-tor,   *let him be heard.*
Plur. Aud-īmĭni, aud-īmĭnor, *Be ye heard.*
aud-iuntor,   *let them be heard.*

SUBJUNCTIVE, OR POTENTIAL MOOD.

1. Present Tense.—*may, can, would, should be.*

Sing. Aud-iar,   *I may be heard.*
aud-iāris, *v.* aud-iāre,   *you may be heard.*
aud-iātur,   *he may be heard.*
Plur. Aud-iāmur,   *We may be heard.*
aud-iāmĭni,   *ye may be heard.*
aud-iantur,   *they may be heard.*

2. Imperfect Tense.—*might be.*

Sing. Aud-īrer,   *I might be heard.*
aud-īrēris, *v.* aud-īrēre,   *you might be heard.*
aud-īrētur,   *he might be heard.*
Plur. Aud-īrēmur,   *We might be heard.*
aud-īrēmĭni,   *ye might be heard.*
aud-īrentur,   *they might be heard.*

3. Perfect Tense.—*may have been.*

Sing. Audīt-us sim, *v.* fuĕrim,   *I may have been heard.*
audīt-us sis, *v.* fuĕris,   *you may have been heard.*
audit-us sit, *v.* fuĕrit,   *he may have been heard.*
Plur. Audīt-i sīmus, *v.* fuĕrĭmus, *We may have been heard.*
audīt-i sītis, *v.* fuĕrītis,   *ye may have been heard.*
audīt-i sint, *v.* fuĕrint,   *they may have been heard.*

4. Pluperfect Tense.—*would, might, could have been.*

Sing. Audīt-us essem, *v.* fuissem,   *I would have been heard.*
     audīt-us esses, *v.* fuisses,   *you would have been heard.*
     audīt-us esset, *v.* fuisset,   *he would have been heard.*
Plur. Audīt-i essēmus,*v.*fuissēmus,*We would have been heard.*
     audīt-i essētis, *v.* fuissētis,   *ye would have been heard.*
     audīt-i essent, *v.* fuissent,   *they would have been heard.*

INFINITIVE MOOD.

Present Tense.

Aud-īri,   *to be heard.*

Perfect and Pluperfect Tense.

Audīt-um esse, *vel* fuisse,   *to have been heard.*

Future Tense.

Audīt-um īri,   *to be about to be heard.*

PARTICIPLES.

The Perfect Tense.

Audīt-us,   *heard,* or, *being heard.*

The Participle in *dus*, or gerundive.

Audien-dus,   *to be heard.*

The two Participles future, in *rus* and in *dus*, are often so combined with the tenses of *sum*, that a new conjugation called the *periphrastic* conjugation is formed in the following manner:—

ACTIVE.

Pres.   Amaturus sum, etc.   *I am about to love.*
Imperf. Amaturus eram, etc.   *I was about to love.*
Perf.   Amaturus fui, etc.   *I have been about to love.*
Pluperf. Amaturus fueram, etc.*I had been about to love.*
1st Fut. Amaturus ero, etc.   *I shall be about to love.*
2nd Fut. Amaturus fuero, etc. *I shall have been about to love.*

And the other moods are formed from the indicative, as is shewn in the conjugation of *sum:*

PASSIVE.

Pres.	Amandus sum,	*I am meet to be loved.*
Imperf.	Amandus eram,	*I was meet to be loved.*
Perf.	Amandus fui,	*I have been meet to be loved.*
Pluperf.	Amandus fueram,	*I had been meet to be loved.*
1st Fut.	Amandus ero,	*I shall be meet to be loved.*
2nd Fut.	Amandus fuero,	*I shall have been meet to be loved.*

DEPONENT verbs are conjugated in this manner:

Hortor, hortāris *v.* hortāre, hortātus sum *v.* fui, hortāri; hortandi, hortando, hortandum; hortatum, hortatu; hortans, hortatus, hortaturus, hortandus:

And so in the other conjugations.

From the third person singular of passive verbs an impersonal verb is formed; and this third person passive exists in words which neither have, nor are capable of having, a regular passive voice: as,

Itur, *that is,*
- Itur a me, *I go.*
- Itur a te, *you go.*
- Itur ab illo, *he goes.*
- Itur a nobis, *we go.*
- Itur a vobis, *ye go.*
- Itur ab illis, *they go.*

Itum est, *that is,*
- itum est a me, *I went.*
- itum est a te, *you went.*
- itum est ab illo, *he went.*
- itum est a nobis, *we went.*
- itum est a vobis, *ye went.*
- itum est ab illis, *they went.*

Future.

Eundum est, *that is,*
- Eundum est a me, *I must go.*
- Eundum est a te, *you must go.*
- Eundum est ab illo, *he must go.*
- Eundum est a nobis, *we must go.*
- Eundum est a vobis, *ye must go.*
- Eundum est ab illis, *they must go.*

And so in all other tenses. The pronoun is scarcely ever expressed in Latin with these impersonals, but is left to be inferred from the context; as, Pugnātum est, *they fought;* vivĭtur, *one lives,* etc.

DECLENSION OF VERBS IRREGULAR.

CERTAIN verbs vary from the general rule, and are formed in the manner following:—

1. Possum, pŏtes, pŏtui, posse, pŏtens :* *to be able.*
2. Vŏlo, vis, vŏlui, velle; vŏlendi, vŏlendo, vŏlendum ; vŏlens : *to be willing.*
3. Nōlo, nonvis, nōlui, nolle ; nōlendi, nōlendo, nōlendum ; nōlens : *to be unwilling.*
4. Mālo, māvis, mālui, malle ; mālendi, mālendo, mālendum ; mālens : *to be more willing,* or, *to have rather,*
5. Ĕdo, ĕdis, *vel* ĕs, ēdi, ĕdĕre *vel* esse : ĕdendi, ĕdendo, ĕdendum ; ēsum, ēsu ; ĕdens, ēsurus : *to eat.*
6. Fĕro, fers, tŭli, ferre ; fĕrendi, fĕrendo, fĕrendum ; lātum, lātu ; fĕrens, lātūrus : *to bear,* or, *suffer.*
7. Fīo, fis, factus sum *vel* fui, fĭĕri ; factus, făciendus : *to be made,* or, *done.*
8. Fĕror, ferris *vel* ferre, lātus sum *vel* fui, ferri; lātus, fĕrendus : *to be borne,* or, *suffered.*

INDICATIVE MOOD.

1. Present Tense.—*I am able,* &c.

Singular.			*Plural.*		
Possum,	pŏtes,	pŏtest,	Possŭmus,	potestis,	possunt.
Vŏlo,	vis,	vult,	vŏlŭmus,	vultis,	vŏlunt.
Nōlo,	nonvis,	nonvult,	nōlŭmus,	nonvultis,	nōlunt.
Mālo,	māvis,	māvult,	mālŭmus,	māvultis,	mālunt.
Ĕdo,	ĕdis, *v.* es,	ĕdit, *v.* est,	ĕdĭmus,	ĕdĭtis,*v.*estis,ĕdunt.	
Fĕro,	fers,	fert,	fĕrĭmus,	fertis,	fĕrunt.
Fīo,	fis,	fit,	fīmus,	fitis,	fiunt.
Fĕror,	ferris, *v.* ferre, fertur,		fĕrĭmur,	ferimĭni,	feruntur.

---

*Potens is, however, only actually used as an adjective, in the sense of *powerful.*

2. Imperfect Tense.—*I was able*, &c.

	Singular.			*Plural.*	
Pŏt-ĕram,	ĕras	ĕrat,	ĕrāmus,	ĕrātis,	ĕrant.
Vŏlē-bam, ⎫ Nōlē-bam, ⎪ Mālē-bam, ⎬ bas, Ĕdē-bam, ⎪ Fĕrē-bam, ⎪ Fīē-bam, ⎭		bat,	bāmus,	bātis,	bant.
Fĕrē-bar, bāris, *v.* bāre, bātur,			bāmur,	bāmĭni,	bantur.

3. Perfect Tense.—*I have been able*, &c.

	Singular.			*Plural.*	
Pŏtu-i, ⎫ Vŏlu-i, ⎪ Nŏlu-i, ⎬ , isti, Mălu-i, ⎪ Ĕd-i, ⎪ Tŭl-i, ⎭		it,	ĭmus,	istis,	ērunt, *vel* ēre.
Fact-us, ⎫ sum, es, *v. v.* Lăt-us, ⎭ fui; fuisti;		est, *v.* fuit;	i sŭmus, estis, sunt, *v.* fuērunt, *v. v. v.* fuĭmus; fuistis; fuēre.		

4. Pluperfect Tense.—*I had been able*, &c.

	Singular.			*Plural.*	
Pŏtu-ĕram, ⎫ Vŏlu-ĕram, ⎪ Nŏlu-ĕram, ⎬ ĕras, Mălu-ĕram, ⎪ Ĕd-ĕram, ⎪ Tŭl-ĕram, ⎭		ĕrat,	ĕrāmus,	ĕrātis,	ĕrant.
Fāct-us, ⎫ ĕram, ĕras, *v. v.* Lāt-us, ⎭ fuĕram;-ĕras;		ĕrat, *v.* -ĕrat;	i ĕrāmus, ĕrātis, ĕrant, *v. v. v.* fuĕrāmus; fuĕrātis; fuĕrant.		

5. First Future Tense.—*I shall, or, will be able,* &c.

	Singular.			Plural.	
Pŏt-ĕro,	ĕris,	ĕrit,	ĕrĭmus,	ĕrĭtis,	ĕrunt.
Vŏl-am, Nōl-am, Māl-am, Ĕd-am, Fĕr-am, Fī-am,	es,	et,	ēmus,	ētis,	ent.
Fĕr-ar,	ĕris, *v.* ēre,	ētur,	ēmur,	ēmĭni,	entur.

6. Second Future, or Future Perfect Tense.—*I shall have been able.*

	Singular.			Plural.	
Pŏtuĕro, Vŏluĕro, Nōluĕro, Māluĕro, Ĕdĕro, Tŭlĕro,	ĕris,	ĕrit,	ĕrĭmus,	ĕrĭtis,	ĕrint.
Factus, *v.* Lātus,	ĕro, *v.* fuĕro,	ĕris, *v.* fuĕris,	ĕrit, *v.* fuĕrit,	Facti, *v.* Lati,	ĕrĭmus, ĕrĭtis, ĕrunt, *v.* fuĕrĭmus, fuĕrĭtis, fuĕrint.

IMPERATIVE MOOD.

Obs. *Possum, volo,* and *malo,* have no Imperative Mood.

Present Tense.—*be thou unwilling,* &c.

Singular.	Plural.
Nŏli, nōlĭto ;	nōlĭte, nōlĭtōte.
Ĕde, ĕdĭto, *vel* Es, esto ; ĕdĭto, *vel,* esto ;	ĕdĭte, ĕdĭtōte, *vel,* este, estote ; ĕdunto.
Fer, ferto ; ferto ;	ferte, fertote ; ferunto.
Fi, fito ; fito ;	fite, fitote ; fiunto.
Fer-re, -tor ; fertor ;	fĕrĭmĭn-i, -or ; feruntor.

SUBJUNCTIVE, OR POTENTIAL MOOD.

1. Present Tense.—*I may be able,* &c.

	Singular.			Plural.	
Poss-im, Věl-im, Nōl-im, Māl-im,	is,	it,	īmus,	ītis,	int.
Ĕd-am, Fĕr-am, Fī-am,	as,	at,	āmus,	ātis,	ant.
Fĕr-ar,	-āris, *v.* āre ; ātur,		āmur,	āmĭni,	antur.

2. Imperfect Tense.—*I might be able,* &c.

	Singular.			Plural.	
Poss-em, Vell-em, Noll-em, Mall-em, Edĕr-em, *vel,* Ess-em, Ferr-em, Fĭĕr-em,	es,	et,	ēmus,	ētis,	ent.
Ferr-er,	-ēris, *v.* ēre ; ētur,		ēmur,	ēmĭni,	entur.

3. Perfect Tense.—*I may have been able,* &c

	Singular.			Plural.	
Pŏtu-ĕrim, Vŏlu-ĕrim, Nōlu-ĕrim, Mālu-ĕrim, Ēd-ĕrim, Tŭl-ĕrim,	ĕris,	ĕrit,	ĕrĭmus,	ĕrĭtis,	ĕrint.
Fact-us,	sim, *v.*	sis, *v.*	sit, *v.*	i sīmus, *v.*	sītis, *v.*	sint, *v.*
Lāt-us,	fuĕ-rim; ris; rit ;		fuĕrĭmus ;	fuĕrĭtis ;	fuĕrint.

4. Pluperfect Tense.—*I should have been able*, &c.

Singular.			Plural.		
Pŏtu-issem,					
Vŏlu-issem,					
Nōlu-issem,	isses,	isset,	issemus,	issētis,	issent.
Mālu-issem,					
Ēd-issem,					
Tŭl-issem,					
Fact-us,	essem, esses, esset,		i essēmus,	essētis,	essent,
	v. *v.* *v.*		*v.*	*v.*	*v.*
Lāt-us,	fuissem; isses; isset;		fuissēmus;	fuissētis;	fuissent.

5. Future Tense.—*I may be about to eat*, &c.

Ēsurus	sim,	sis,	sit,	i sīmus,	sītis,	sint.
Lātūrus						

INFINITIVE MOOD.

Present Tense.—*to be able*, &c.

Posse.   Ĕdĕre, *vel,* esse.
Velle.   Ferre.
Nolle.   Fĭĕri.
Malle.   Ferri.

Perfect and Pluperfect Tense.—*to have been able*, &c.

Pŏtuisse.   Ēdisse.
Vŏluisse.   Tŭlisse.
Nōluisse.   Factum esse, *vel,* fuisse.
Māluisse.   Lātum esse, *vel,* fuisse.

Future Tense.—*to be about to eat*, &c.

Ēsūrum esse.   Factum iri.
Lātūrum esse.   Lātum iri.

Obs. *Possum, volo, nolo, malo,* have no Future Tense of the Infinitive mood.

EO, to go, is also a verb irregular.

Eo, is, *īvi, īre, eundi, eundo, eundum, ĭtum, ĭtu, iens, ĭtūrus.

Indic. M. } Sing. Eo, is, it.   *Pl.* Imus, ītis, eunt.
Pres. T.

---

* In all the compounds of *eo,* as *redeo, abeo,* etc. this tense is almost invariably found *ii,* not *ivi;* as, *redii, abii* etc.

Imp. Tense. Sing. Ibam, ības, ībat. *Pl.*-āmus, -ātis, -ant.
Perf. Tense. Ivi, ivisti, ivit; ivimus, ivistis, ivērunt, *v.* ēre.
Pluperf. Tense. Ivĕram, -as, -at ; -āmus, -ātis, -ant.
First Fut. Sing. Ibo, ībis, ībit. *Pl.*-īmus, -ĭtis, -unt.
2nd Fut. Ivĕro, īvĕris, īvĕrit ; īvĕrīmus, īvĕrītis, īvĕrint.
Imp. M. Sing. I, ito ; ito. *Pl.* īte, itote ; eunto.
Potent. M. Pres. Sing. Eam, eas, eat. *Pl.* Eamus, eātis,
    Imperf. Irem, *etc.* [eant.
    Perf. Ivĕrim, *etc.*
    Pluperf. Ivissem, *etc.*
    Fut. Iturus sim, *etc.*
    Gerunds ; Eundi, eundo, eundum.
    Participle Pres. T. Iens, *gen.* eüntis.
    Participle Future, Itūrus.*

Obs. In like manner are the compounds of *Eo* declined, also *queo,* to be able, and *nequeo,* to be unable ; except that these last two have no Imperative mood or Gerunds.

DEFECTIVE VERBS.

VERBS are called *defective,* that have only some particular Tenses and Persons ; as,
Aio, *I say.*
Ind. M. Pres. T. S. Aio, ais, ait. *Pl.* —— Aiunt.
Imp. T. Sing. Aiē-bam, -bas, -bat. *Pl.* -bamus, -batis,
    -bant.
Perf. Tense. Sing. — Ait.
Sub. or *Potent. M. Pres. T. Sing.*—Aias, aiat. *Pl.* aiant.
    Particip. Pres. Tense. Aiens.
FARI, *to speak.*
Pres. 3d. Sing. Fātur.
Perf. Fātus sum, es, *etc.*
Pluperf. Fātus eram, *etc.*
First Fut. Fābor— no other person.

---

* *Eo* has no passive voice except in the third sing. used as an impersonal verb, as has been shewn above (p. 57,) and the passive participle in *dus,* or gerundive *eundus* ; but some of its compounds, *ădeo,* to approach, *prætereo,* to pass by, &c. have a passive voice, formed regularly from the active ; as, *adeor, adiris, aditur,* etc. imperf. *adibar,* etc.

Imper. Fāre.
Gerunds. Fandi, Fando.
Supine. Fatu. — *Part. Perf.* Fatus. — *Part. Pass.*
[Fandus.

Āve, *Hail!*
  Imper. M. Sing.—Āve, ăvēto.—*Pl.* Āvēte, ăvētōte.—
  Infinitive Mood. Āvēre.
Salve, *Hail!*
  Indicat. M. Future T. Sing. — Salvēbis.
  Imper. M. S.—Salve, salveto.—*Pl.* Salvēte, salvētōte.
  Infinitive M. Salvēre.
Cedo, *Give me.*
  Imper. M. Sing.—Cĕdo.—*Pl.*—Cette.*
Quæso, *I pray.*
  Indic. M. Pres. T. S. Quæso. *Pl.* Quæsŭmus.
Inquam, *I say.*
  Ind. M. Pres. T. S. Inquam, -quis, -quit. *Pl.* Inquĭmus, inquĭtis, inquiunt.
  Preterimp. T. S.—Inquiebat. *Pl.*—Inquiebant.
  Preterp. T. S. —Inquisti.
  Future T. Sing.—Inquies, inquiet.

Cœpi, I have begun, *memĭni,* I remember, *nōvi,* I know, *odi,* I hate, are perfects of obsolete presents, (except *novi,* which is also the perfect of *nosco,)* and have these tenses only which are derived from the perfect. Their pluperfect tense has the sense of the imperfect; i.e. *memineram,* "I did remember," not, "I had remembered," etc. and the second future has the sense of the first future; as, *odero* "I shall hate," not "I shall have hated."

Cœpi,   Mĕmĭni,   (So, ōdi, nōvi.)
Cœpisti,   Mĕmĭnisti,
Cœpit,   Mĕmĭnit,
Cœpĭmus,   Mĕmĭnĭmus,
Cœpistis,   Mĕmĭnistis,
Cœperunt, *v.* ēre. Mĕmĭnērunt, *v.* ēre.

---

* Found only in the oldest writers.

Pluperf. Cœpĕram, nemĭnĕram, ōdĕram, nōvĕram.
Future. Cœpĕro, memĭnĕro, ōdĕro, nōvĕro.
Imper. Mĕmento, mĕmentōte.—The other verbs have no imperative.
Potent. Perf. Cœpĕrim, memĭnĕrim, ōdĕrim, nōvĕrim.
Pluperf. Cœpissem, meminissem, odissem, novissem.
Infin. Cœpisse, memĭnisse, ōdisse, nōvisse.
Part. fut. act. Cœpturus, ōsūrus.—The others have no participle.
Perf. part. pass. Cœptus.

Ausim, I may dare, an old form of the present subjunctive of *audeo*.
Ausim, ausis, ausit;——ausint.

Faxim, I may do, a similar form from *facio*.
Faxim, faxis, faxit; faximus, faxitis, faxint.
Fut. faxo.

ADVERBS.

An *Adverb* is a part of speech joined to verbs and nouns adjective (sometimes even to other adverbs) to qualify them; as, *lŏquĭtur bĕne*, he speaks well; *scrībunt măle*, they write badly.*

CONJUNCTIONS.

A *Conjunction* is a part of speech which joins sentences or words together: some connect things of the same kind, and are called *copulative conjunctions*; some connect things which are distinct from each other, and are called *disjunctive conjunctions*.—The copulative conjunctions are *et, ac, atque, necnon*, " and," *nĕque*, " nor," *quàm*, " than."—The disjunctive conjunctions are *aut, vel, ve, sīve, seu,* " or."

---

* When derived from adjectives, adverbs have comparative and superlative degrees, formed from the corresponding degrees of the adjectives; as, from *doctus* learned, *doctior, doctissimus,* are derived *docte* learnedly, *doctius* more learnedly, *doctissime* most learnedly.

F 3

PREPOSITIONS.

A *Preposition* is a part of speech which governs a case, and which expresses the relation of nouns to one another, or to verbs; as, *iter per Italiam*, a journey through Italy; *exit e domo*, he goes out of the house.

These Prepositions have an *Accusative* case after them:

Ad, to.
Adversum, Adversus, against, towards.
Ante, before.
Apud, at, or near.
Circa, circum, about.
Circĭter, about (of time, or number.)
Cis, citra, on this side.
Contra, against.
Erga, towards.
Extra, without.
Infra, beneath, below.
Inter, between, or among.
Intra, within.
Juxta, beside, or near to.
Ob, on account of, before, (as *ob oculos*, before the eyes.)
Pĕnes, in the power of.
Per, through.
Pōne, behind.
Post, after.
Præter, besides, except, before (as, *præter cæteros*, before others.)
Prŏpe, (and compar. and superl. *prŏpius, proxime*) nigh, or near to.
Propter, on account of, near to.
Sĕcundum, according to.
Supra, above.
Trans, on the further side.
Versus, towards.
Ultra, beyond.

The Prepositions following have an *Ablative* case after them:

A, (and before vowels *ab*,)* from, by.
Absque, without.
Coram, before, or in presence of.
Cum, with.
De, from, concerning.
E, ex, from, out of, in (as *ex ordine*, in order.)
Præ,† before, in comparison of, on account of.
Pro, for, in front of.
Sine, without.
Tĕnus, up to, as far as.‡

---

* Before *te, abs* is also used in the same sense by Cicero, and before other words by Terence and older writers. It is never used in poetry.

† *Præ* signifies of *place*, with verbs of motion only, and with pronouns.

‡ *Tenus* is used also with a genitive, when the noun is in the plural number; and once by Livy with a noun in the singular; *Corcȳræ tĕnus*, as far as Corcyra.

The prepositions *versus* and *tenus* are always, *penes* sometimes, put after the noun governed by them: so, when the noun governed by them is the relative, *ante*, *contra*, *inter*, and *propter*, are also placed sometimes after their case: when *cum* is joined with *me, nobis, te, vobis, se*, or the relative, it is put after them, and united with them so as to make one word; as, *mecum, vobiscum, quocum*, etc.

The Prepositions following have either an Accusative or an Ablative case after them:

In, for *into*, signifying motion *towards, against, over*, etc. has an accusative case; as, *Eo in urbem*, I go into the city.

In, meaning "in," has the ablative case; as, *In illo spes est*, my hope is in him.

Sub, after verbs of motion, governs an accusative case, and also when it denotes time; as, *Mittitur sub jugum*, he is sent under the yoke; *sub noctem*, about nightfall. When it means "under," it governs an ablative case; as, *Sub terrâ*, under the earth.

Subter, under, beneath, governs the accusative; the ablative only in poetry; (it is very rarely used at all.)

Super, when it means "on, above, besides," governs the accusative case; as, *Super terram*, above the earth: when it means "concerning, about," it governs the ablative; as, *Rogitans multa super Priamo*, asking many things about Priam.

Besides these regular prepositions, some adverbs are used occasionally as prepositions, especially in poetry.

With the Accusative:

Usque (properly, and more usually, in good prose invariably, *usque ad*,) as far as.

With the Ablative:

Palam, in the presence of.
Procul, (properly, and more usually, *procul a*,) far from.
Simul, (only poetically for *simul cum*,) together with.

With the Accusative or Ablative:

Clam, without the knowledge of, (the accusative, however, is very rare and antiquated.)

OF AN INTERJECTION.

An Interjection is a part of speech which betokens a sudden motion of the mind, be it grief, or joy, or other passion.

THE THREE CONCORDS EXPLAINED.

There are three Concords, or Agreements, in Latin:
1. Between the nominative case and the verb.
2. Between the substantive and the adjective.
3. Between the antecedent and the relative.

THE FIRST CONCORD.

A Verb agrees with its nominative case in number and person.

In order to find out the nominative case, ask the question *who*, or *what?* with the verb; and the word that answers to the question, is the nominative case to the verb; as, *who reads? who regard not?*

The *master* reads, but *ye* regard not,
ᵃ*Præceptor* ᵇ*legit,* ᵃ*vos verò* ᵇ*negligitis.*

Sometimes the infinitive mood of a verb is used as a neuter substantive in the nominative, in which case the verb agrees with that, as if it were a noun; as,

Diluculò ᵃ*surgere saluberrimum* ᵇ*est,*
To rise betimes in the morning is most wholesome.

When two or more substantives are so joined in one sentence, that the verb depends on both or on all of them, the verb is usually put in the plural number, and agrees especially with the nominative case of the most worthy person:* when, however, the nouns denote things, not persons, the verb is often kept in the singular number; as, *Ego et tu sumus in tuto,* I and you are in safety: *Cùm tempus necessitasque postulat,* when time and necessity require.

---

* In grammatical language, the first person is reckoned more worthy than the second, and the second than the third.

Sometimes also a noun of multitude, (that is, a noun expressing more persons or things than one,) though in the singular number itself, is followed by a verb in the plural number; as, *Turba ruunt,* the crowd rushes on. When the nominative case to the verb is a personal pronoun, it is usually omitted in Latin, unless particular emphasis be desired; as, He governs France, *Regit Galliam :* I am wiser than you, *Ego sum te sapientior.*

THE SECOND CONCORD.

The adjective agrees with its substantive in case, gender, and number; as,

a*Amicus* b *certus in* a *re* b *incertâ cernitur,*
A sure friend is tried in a doubtful matter.

When two or more substantives come together in one sentence, and have one adjective referring to all of them, the adjective is put in the plural number, and as to gender agrees with the substantive of the most worthy gender, (the masculine being accounted more worthy than the feminine, and the feminine more worthy than the neuter.) But, when the nouns denote things, the adjective is often put in the neuter; when they denote both persons and things, the adjective may either agree with the noun denoting the person, or be put in the neuter gender; as, *Mihi păter et māter mortui sunt,* my father and mother are dead : *Ira et ăvārĭtia pŏtentia sunt,* anger and avarice are powerful.

Sometimes the infinitive mood of a verb is used as a noun of the neuter gender, and the adjective agrees with it as if it were such a noun; and sometimes an entire sentence supplies the place of the substantive, and the adjective which is applied to it is put in the neuter gender; as, *Errāre hūmānum est,* to err is human.

Sometimes, when persons are denoted by neuter substantives, the adjective, nevertheless, is put in the masculine or feminine gender; as, *Millia trīginta servōrum capti sunt,* thirty thousand slaves were taken.

When in English the word *man,* or *thing,* is put with an adjective, you may in Latin leave out the substantive, and put the adjective in the masculine or neuter gender; as,

Multi falluntur, many men are deceived.
Multa me impediērunt, many things have hindered me.

THE THIRD CONCORD.

When you have a relative, ask this question, *who,* or *what?* with the verb; and the word that answereth to the question, shall be the antecedent to the relative.

The relative agrees with its antecedent in gender, number, and person; as,

a *Vir sapit,* b *qui pauca loquitur,*
The man is wise, *who* speaketh few words.

If the relative refers to two antecedents, or more, then it is put in the plural number; and if they be of different persons, the relative agrees with the antecedent of the more worthy person; as, *Ego et tu qui ĕrāmus dŏmi,* I and you who were at home.

Sometimes a sentence supplies the place of the antecedent, and in this case the relative is put in the neuter gender; as, *In tempŏre vēni, quod rērum omnium est prīmum,* I came in time, which is the most important thing of all.

When the relative is placed between two substantives, to both of which it refers, it commonly agrees with the latter; as, *Anĭmal quem vŏcāmus hŏmĭnem,* the animal which we call man.

February, 1879.

BOOKS
PRINTED AT
THE ETON COLLEGE PRESS:
PUBLISHED BY

Messrs. WILLIAMS AND SON, Eton College;

AND TO BE HAD ALSO OF

MESSRS. SIMPKIN, MARSHALL, & CO. London.

VERSE BOOKS.

CLIVUS: Exercises in Latin Elegiac Verse, Part I, Full Sense. Compiled by A. C. Ainger, Esq., M. A., Assistant Master at Eton College .... *Crown 8vo., cloth, Price*, 2s. 6d.

NUCIPRUNA: Exercises in Latin Elegiac Verse grafted on "Nuces," by the Rev. Herbert Kynaston, *M. A.*, Principal of Cheltenham College........................... *Crown 8vo., Price* 1s.

*A Key to the above by the Rev. H. Kynaston, *M. A.*, ...*Cr. 8vo.*, 2s.

LUCRETILIS: an Introduction to the Art of Writing Latin Lyric Verses, in Two Parts, by the Author of "Nuces." Second Edition of both Parts .... *Crown 8vo.*, *each* 1s.

* A KEY to the above, by the Author .... *Crown 8vo. Price* 2s.

IONIDES: Exercises in Greek Iambics, with a Vocabulary, by the Rev. E. D. Stone, M. A., late Fellow of King's College, Cambridge, Assistant Master at Eton College. *Cr. 8vo., Price* 1s.

IAMBIC EXERCISES, based on the Prometheus Vinctus, by the Rev. E. D. Stone, *M. A.* ...*Crown 8vo, (uniform with [the above), Price* 6d,

* *To be had* only *of the Publishers.*

VERSE RULES FOR BEGINNERS, by the Author of "Nuces." on Card, 2pp., Large 8vo., *Price* 4d.

A SIMPLE PROSODY, intended chiefly for Beginners; *Crown 8vo.*, Twelfth Edition............................*Price* 3d.

LATIN EXERCISE BOOKS.

NUCES: Exercises on the Syntax of the Public School Latin Primer. In Three Parts. Part I., Eleventh Thousand; Part II., Eighth Thousand; Part III., Seventh Thousand. Used in the Fourth Form at Eton.......................*Crown 8vo., each* 1s.

The Three Parts may also be had Bound together in Cloth, Price 3s.

HINTS FOR LATIN PROSE, by an Eton Master;

LATIN BOOKS.

OVID LESSONS, being Easy Passages selected from the Elegiac Poems of Ovid and Tibullus, with Explanatory (English) Notes by HENRY GILBERT WINTLE, M.A., Assistant Master at Eton College. .... *Crown 8vo., cloth, Price* 2s. 6d.

THE HANNIBALIAN OR SECOND PUNIC WAR, Extracted from the Third Decade of Livy, with English Notes by the Rev. E. D. STONE, M.A., Late Fellow of King's College, Cambridge; Assistant Master at Eton....*Cr. 8vo., cl., Price* 3s.

YONGE'S LATIN GRAMMAR; (originally compiled for use at Eton, and still used in many Grammar Schools) 12mo. *cl.* 2s.

YONGE'S LATIN ACCIDENCE; the above Grammar to the end of the Conjugation of Verbs .... 12mo. *cl.* 1s.

ELECTA EX OVIDIO ET TIBULLO; with English Notes explanatory and illustrative, by Rev. W. G. COOKESLEY, M.A. (late Assistant Master at Eton.) Thirtieth Thousand.
12mo. *cl.* 3s. 6d.

OVIDII EPISTOLÆ; (containing the Epistles *not* in the above Selections,) BURMANN'S Text............... 12mo. *cl.* 2s. 6d.

CÆSAR'S GALLIC WAR; First Six Books, with English Notes by Rev. W. G. COOKESLEY, M.A. (late Assistant Master at Eton.) With Maps, by WELLER, of Gaul and the first Four Campaigns. Ninth Thousand..................... 12mo. *cl.* 3s. 6d.

CATULLI CARMINA SELECTA; with English Notes by Rev. W. G. COOKESLEY, M.A. (late Assistant Master at Eton.)
12mo. *cl.* 2s. 6d.

SCRIPTORES ROMANI; Selections from Cicero, Livy, Tacitus, Quintilian, Pliny, and Paterculus...... 8vo. *half-bound,* 4s.
cloth 3s.

GREEK BOOKS.

POETÆ GRÆCI, Extracts from the less Familiar Epic, Lyric, Elegiac, Philosophic, Dramatic, and Bucolic Poets of Greece, from Hesiod to Gætulicus, with English Notes by Rev. HERBERT KYNASTON, M.A., Principal of Cheltenham College; sometime Fellow of St. John's College, Cambridge, and Assistant Master at Eton .... *Crown 8vo., cloth, Price*

SERTUM; A Greek Reading Book, with English Notes. Eighth Thousand. Used in the Fourth Form at Eton.
Cr. 8vo. *cl.* 2s. 6d.

HINTS AND CAUTIONS ON ATTIC GREEK PROSE COMPOSITION, by the Rev. F. St. J. THACKERAY, M.A., late Fellow of Lincoln College, Oxford, Assistant Master at Eton College............................*Cr. 8vo., cloth, Price* 3s. 6d.

EXERCISES ON THE IRREGULAR AND DEFECTIVE GREEK VERBS, by the Rev. F. St. J. THACKERAY, M.A., late Fellow of Lincoln College, Oxford, Assistant Master at Eton College (Second Edition) .. *Demy 8vo., cloth, Price* 2s.

KEY to the above (to be had *only* of the Publishers.)
Crown 8vo, Price 2s. 6d.

GREEK BOOKS (continued.)

SELECTA EX HERODOTO (used in the Lower Fifth.)
Demy 8vo, cloth, Price 2s. 6d.

THE ETON GREEK GRAMMAR..............12mo. cl. 4s.

PART I. OF THE ABOVE; Rudimenta Minora...12mo. cl. 2s.

PART II.   „   „   Syntaxis............12mo. cl. 2s.

ST. MATTHEW'S GOSPEL, Used in the Fourth Form.
Crown 8vo. cl. 1s. 9d.

ÆSOPI FABULÆ, GR. ET LAT.; (the Latin Translation may be omitted, as at Eton,) with Latin Notes by an Eton Master. ....12mo. cl. 3s.

PINDARI CARMINA, Part I.; Odæ Olymp. *(Out of Print.)*
„   „   Part II.; Odæ Pythiæ 8vo. 7s. 6d.
„   „   Part III.; Nemeææ et Isthmiæ 7s. 6d.
„   „   Part IV.; Fragmenta et Index, 7s. 6d.

With English Notes by Rev. W. G. Cookesley, M.A., (late Assistant Master at Eton.)

FRENCH BOOKS.

THE ETON FIRST FRENCH READING BOOK; being a new and thoroughly revised Edition of Tarver's "New Method," by H. & F. Tarver, Esqs.(Third Ed.) Cr.8vo. cl. 3s.6d.

THE ETON FRENCH ACCIDENCE & FIRST FRENCH EXERCISE BOOK, with Vocabularies, by H. Tarver, Esq. (French Master at Eton.) Third Edition...........12mo. cl. 4s.

ARITHMETIC.

FRACTIONS, &c. ENLARGED; by Rev. H. Daman, M.A., Assistant Master at Eton, late Mathematical Master at Magdalen College School, Oxford ....Crown 8vo. cloth, 2s.

The aim of the writer has been to produce a Text-Book on Unapplied Arithmetic containing, besides Examples, explanations and directions suitable to ordinary School-boys.

ENUNCIATIONS OF EUCLID: Books I. to IV.
Cr. 8vo, Price 4d.

EUCLID, Book I, Propositions 1 to 26, with Exercises on each Proposition, and Alternative Proofs for some of the more difficult Theorems, by an Eton Master....*Demy 8vo., cloth,*
[Price 1s. 6d.

MISCELLANEOUS.

GEOMETRY IN MODERN LIFE: being the substance of Two Lectures on Useful Geometry given before the Literary Society at Eton, by J. Scott-Russell, Esq., M. A., F. R. S.
[Demy 8vo., cloth, Price 3s. 6d.

ETON SELECTIONS FROM OVID AND TIBULLUS Translated into English Verse, by the Rev. H. W. Hodgson, M.A., Rector of Ashwell, in the County of Hertford, and formerly of Balliol College, Oxford....*Cr. 8vo., cl., Price 3s. 6d.*

MISCELLANEOUS *(continued.)*

THE ETON PORTRAIT GALLERY, consisting of Short Memoirs of the More Eminent Eton Men, by a BARRISTER OF THE INNER TEMPLE; with Twelve Steel Engravings, designed and executed by Cavalier GABRIELLI.

Demy 8vo., Price 18s., India Paper, 21s.

A few Large Paper copies (India Proofs) of the Engravings can be had in a Portfolio, Price £2 2s.

FAMILY PRAYERS FOR ONE WEEK, by the Rev. Pownoll W. PHIPPS, M A., Vicar of Upton-cum-Chalvey.

Cr. 8vo., cl., Price 1s.

THE ETON SCHOOL LIST; Published at the commencement and end of each School-time...............8vo., Price 6d.

THE ETON ALMANACK; Published at the commencement of each School-time........................Demy folio, Price 6d.

GREEK DERIVATION PAPERS,

Fcap. Folio, 4 Forms on a Sheet, per Quire, 2s.

Reduced in Price, to 10s. 6d. cloth; 16s. tree-calf; 20s. morocco plain.

MUSÆ ETONENSES, Sive Carminum Etonæ Conditorum Delectus; being "Sent up" Exercises of, among others, Archbishop Sumner; Bishops Lonsdale, Abraham, Durnford; Selwyn; Provosts Goodford, Hodgson, Hawtrey; Lords Derby, Auckland, Stratford de Redcliffe, Lyttelton; Deans Milman, Wellesley, (*Windsor*); Sirs G. C. Lewis, E. Creasy; and W. E. Gladstone, W. M. Praed, A. H. Hallam, H. H. Knapp.

Edited by DR. OKES, Provost of King's College, Cambridge.

THE ETON BOATING BOOK; Containing an Account of the Races, with List of the Boats from 1825 to 1875, with Lists of the Oxford and Cambridge Crews; by R. H. BLAKE-HUMFREY, Esq., Captain of the Boats 1860 and 1861.

Second Editon Cr. 8vo. cl. 3s. 6d.

THE ETON SCHOOL LISTS, with Appendix, from 1791 to 1860, with Short Notes and Alphabetical Index, by H. E. C. STAPYLTON, Esq.

Second Edition, 4to. *cloth, reduced in price to* 12s. 6d.

APPENDIX to Ditto, (to be had separately,) 1853, 1856, 1859.

4to, cloth, Price 5s

THE ETON COLLEGE CHRONICLE, Published Fortnightly during each School-time, *Price* 3d.; *by Post* 3½d.

Annual Subscription, including Postage, 6s.

INDUSTRY AND IDLENESS: A MORAL CONTRAST, by the Author of a Memoir of B. Bolingbroke Woodward B.A., F.S.A., &c., late Librarian to the Queen.

Fcp. 8vo., Price 1s.

www.ingramcontent.com/pod-product-compliance
Lightning Source LLC
Chambersburg PA
CBHW020241090426
42735CB00010B/1783